CONTENTS

ORIGINS OF THE CAMPAIGN	5
CHRONOLOGY	13
OPPOSING COMMANDERS	15
The British . The Spanish . The French	
OPPOSING FORCES	19
The British . The Spanish . The French . Orders of battle	
OPPOSING PLANS	27
The French . The British and Spanish	
THE TALAVERA CAMPAIGN	39
The area of the coming battle . The battle of Talavera, 27 July	
The battle continues, 28 July . Losses at Talavera	
AFTERMATH	81
French reinforcements on the way . Baños . Napoleon's opinion	
THE BATTLEFIELD TODAY	91
FURTHER READING	94
INDEX	95

CAMPAIGN 253

TALAVERA 1809

Wellington's lightning strike into Spain

RENÉ CHARTRAND ILLUSTRATED BY GRAHAM TURNER
Series editor Marcus Cowper

OSPREY PUBLISHING
Bloomsbury Publishing Plc

PO Box 883, Oxford, OX1 9PL, UK
1385 Broadway, 5th Floor, New York, NY 10018, USA
Email: info@ospreypublishing.com

OSPREY is a trademark of Osprey Publishing, a division of
Bloomsbury Publishing Plc

© 2013 Osprey Publishing

First published in Great Britain in 2013 by Osprey Publishing

Transferred to digital print-on-demand in 2020

All rights reserved. Apart from any fair dealing for the purpose of private study, research, criticism or review, as permitted under the Copyright, Designs and Patents Act, 1988, no part of this publication may be reproduced, stored in a retrieval system, or transmitted in any form or by any means, electronic, electrical, chemical, mechanical, optical, photocopying, recording or otherwise, without the prior written permission of the copyright owner. Enquiries should be addressed to the Publishers.

Printed and bound in Great Britain

ISBN: 978 1 78096 180 4
E-book ISBN: 978 1 78096 181 1
E-pub ISBN: 978 1 78096 182 8

Editorial by Ilios Publishing Ltd, Oxford, UK (www.iliospublishing.com)
Index by Alan Thatcher
Typeset in Myriad Pro and Sabon
Maps by Bounford.com
3D bird's-eye view by The Black Spot
Battlescene illustrations by Graham Turner
Originated by PDQ Media, Bungay, UK

The Woodland Trust
Osprey Publishing supports the Woodland Trust, the UK's leading woodland conservation charity.

www.ospreypublishing.com
To find out more about our authors and books visit our website. Here you will find extracts, author interviews, details of forthcoming events and the option to sign-up for our newsletter.

ACKNOWLEDGEMENTS

I am grateful to Natalia Griffon de Pleineville in Paris and Luis Sorando Muzas in Saragoza, the staff at The National Archives at Kew (UK) and the Anne S.K. Brown Military Collection at the Brown University Library in Providence (USA). All this material could never have come together in a handsome book without the fine editorial work and kind coordination of Marcus Cowper at Osprey. To one and all, I extend my heartfelt expression of deepest gratitude.

AUTHOR'S NOTE

The battle of Talavera is regarded as one of the British victories of the Peninsular War yet it did not stop the invasion and occupation of the Peninsula by Napoleon's troops. The French army's regrettable barbarity towards the Spanish and Portuguese was answered by guerrilla warfare and a national mobilization sacrificing everything to the struggle. Fortunately, to face the invaders, the allies had in Wellesley (the future Duke of Wellington) a truly superior leader. But his British army was never numerous enough to face the French imperial hordes alone. The Spanish army was numerous, but its command was rather confused and much of it was made up of badly trained, haphazardly armed and somewhat undisciplined recent levies. The 1809 Portuguese army could not help greatly as it was in the process of being totally reorganized. The French army sent into Spain was far stronger; part of it was battle-tested and its senior officers were considered the best in the world. Wellesley's daring advance that took his army as far as Talavera and the battle that ensued was, for Napoleon, the first of many 'reality checks' regarding the true worth of his senior officers and their men in the Peninsula.
The spelling of Spanish words generally follows the adaptations that have long been prevalent in British and American military and historical publications, in particular as expressed by Oxford Professor Sir Charles Oman in his *History of the Peninsular War*.

ARTIST'S NOTE

Readers may care to note that the original paintings from which the colour plates in this book were prepared are available for private sale. The Publishers retain all reproduction copyright whatsoever. All enquiries should be addressed to:

Graham Turner, PO Box 568, Aylesbury, Bucks, HP17 8ZX, UK
www.studio88.co.uk

The Publishers regret that they can enter into no correspondence upon this matter.

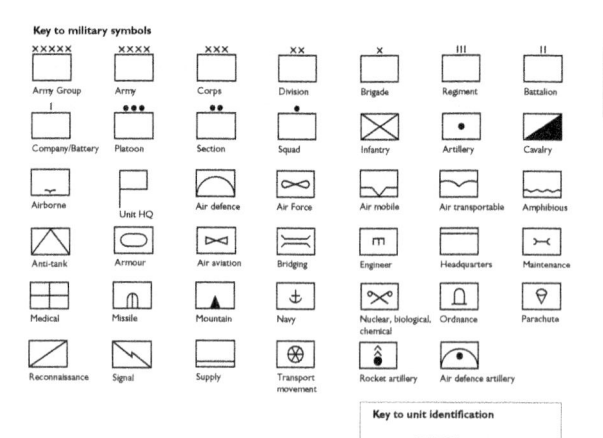

ORIGINS OF THE CAMPAIGN

In the early 19th century, Great Britain was at war with France, which was then led by its emperor crowned in 1804, Napoleon I. Through international trade, Britain had nevertheless become one of the world's most prosperous nations. In order to break its sources of wealth, the French Emperor established, in 1806, a 'Continental Blockade' to cut off Britain's trade with the European mainland. With Napoleon or his allies now in control of nearly all the European coastline, a trade ban with Britain would, he hoped, weaken Britain's economy as well as deny the island nation its vital timber sources from Baltic countries to build ships. This hope of 'naval starvation' was, in fact, being shattered even before Trafalgar; British shipyards had already turned to Canada whose timber exports multiplied by about 20 times in a few years creating unprecedented economic expansion in British North America.

The most severe flaw in Napoleon's Continental Blockade was the reluctance that Portugal entertained to apply it. Portugal was reputed as 'Britain's oldest ally'. Although a neutral country at that time, the blockade meant the ruin of its commerce so trade between Lisbon and London went on, creating a huge gap in the Continental Blockade. Thus Napoleon made the decision to invade and occupy Portugal. To do that, Gen. Andoche Junot leading a French army of 30,000 men was sent into Spain during the autumn of 1807, while the Spanish ally was told to muster at least an equal number of men; all would then march into Portugal, secure the country, and apprehend and destitute its royal family. Ordinary Spaniards who now gazed at tens of thousands of their 'allied' French troops marching across Spain were not reassured. Would they be next?

Portugal could not repel such an invasion force as now massed along its eastern border. Its regular army had, perhaps, 25,000 men of which 10,000 to 15,000 might be fit for service. Worse, its most influential senior officer, the Marquis de Alorna, was pro-French and felt Portugal's long-term salvation would come from becoming part of the pan-European empire mooted by Napoleon. Other generals and some intellectuals also felt there could be no other solution. Even the British estimated that creating a 'front' in Portugal was hopeless. In November, Gen. Junot's army, now regrouped at Alcantara, crossed into Portugal by the narrow mountain passes along the upper Tagus River. It was a daring gamble since a well-entrenched force might have blocked the invaders, but Junot felt that resistance would be nil or minimal and, sure enough, his army marched in, easily brushed off what feeble opposition there was, and progressed towards Lisbon. Meanwhile, Gen. Caraffa's 25,000-strong Spanish contingent entered the north of the country and eventually peacefully occupied Porto.

OPPOSITE
Joseph Bonaparte, King of Spain, 1808–1813. Nominally the commander of the French army at Talavera, but effective command was assumed by marshals Jourdan and Victor. Print from a drawing by Eric Pape after a formal court portrait by François Gérard. (Private collection. Author's photo)

The Iberian Peninsula, early to mid-1809

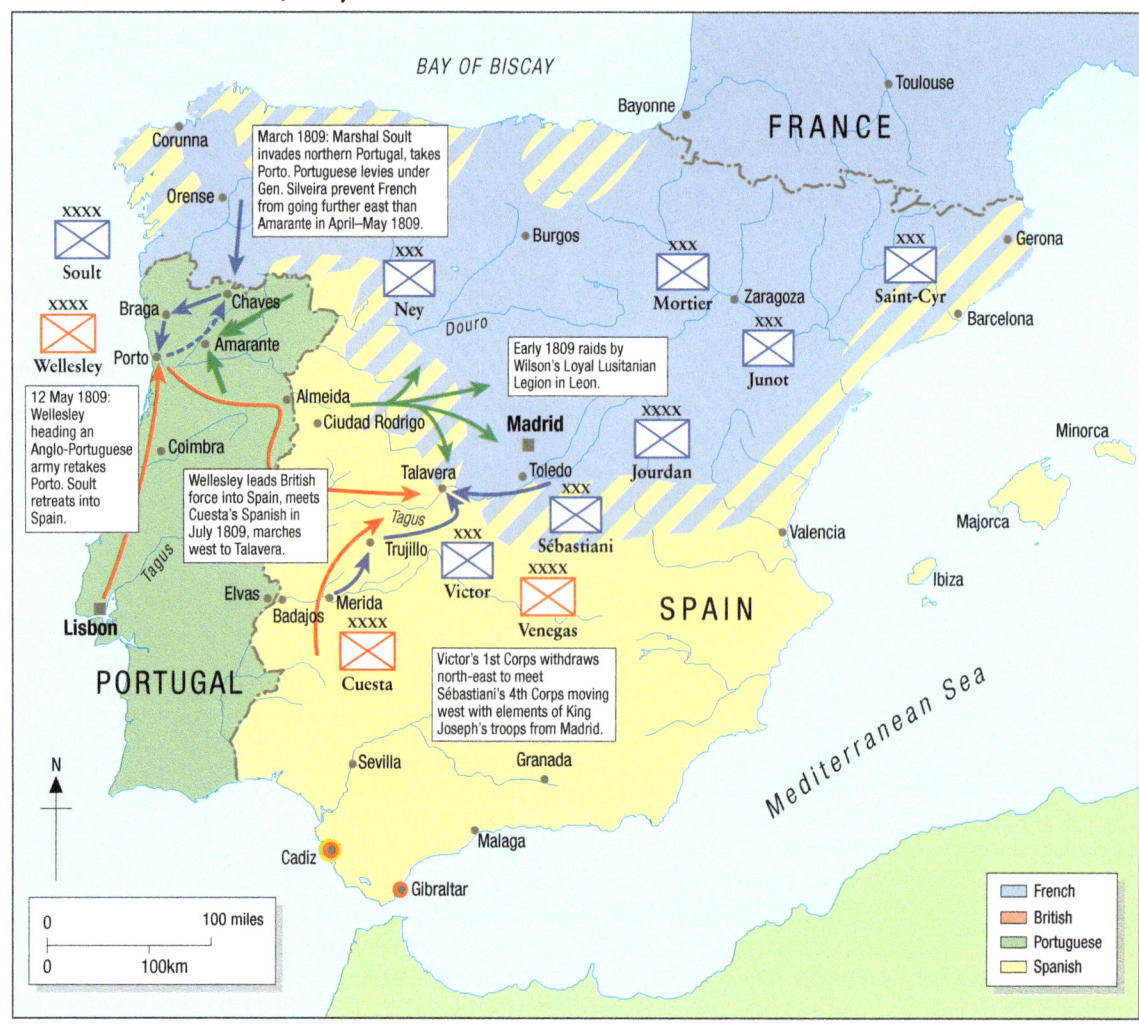

Map annotations:

- **March 1809:** Marshal Soult invades northern Portugal, takes Porto. Portuguese levies under Gen. Silveira prevent French from going further east than Amarante in April–May 1809.
- **12 May 1809:** Wellesley heading an Anglo-Portuguese army retakes Porto. Soult retreats into Spain.
- Early 1809 raids by Wilson's Loyal Lusitanian Legion in Leon.
- Wellesley leads British force into Spain, meets Cuesta's Spanish in July 1809, marches west to Talavera.
- Victor's 1st Corps withdraws north-east to meet Sébastiani's 4th Corps moving west with elements of King Joseph's troops from Madrid.

Legend: French / British / Portuguese / Spanish

In the royal palace at Lisbon, Prince Regent Joao VI knew that the French would soon appear and that any military resistance would cause a needless bloodbath. He would become a prisoner of the French Emperor and his nation would likely be partitioned amongst Napoleon's minions. Faced with this impossible situation, Joao VI made an extraordinary decision that saved the crown and Portugal. Instead of bending his knee to the Emperor Napoleon and his French army, he decided to leave Lisbon and go to Brazil, Portugal's immense territory in America, taking with him the royal family and all those at the royal court that would follow him. On 27 November, Joao VI, with some 15,000 people, embarked on a large fleet that sailed out of the Tagus River.

On 7 March 1808, the residents of Rio de Janeiro saw a large fleet of Portuguese and British warships enter the city's superb harbour. On board the 90-gun ship-of-the-line *Principe Real* was the Prince Regent and the royal family who soon landed to a triumphant welcome. There was no precedent in modern history for such an extraordinary royal gesture, the immediate effects of which were obvious; the legitimate Portuguese government in

Brazil was safe from Napoleon's clutches and no matter what the French did in occupied Portugal, its people's heart and soul would always look towards its true rulers in Rio de Janeiro that no French minions could replace. For Britain, the advantage was obvious; Portugal was henceforth in the war against imperial France and, in time, would prove to be a faithful and outstanding ally.

Indeed, the time was soon to come. Following the occupation of Portugal, Napoleon sent more troops into the Iberian Peninsula so that, by early 1808, at least 70,000 men were in Spain and Portugal. The Emperor's next objective was to get rid of the 'degenerate' Bourbon royal family in Spain and replace it by crowning his brother Joseph as king of Spain 'and of the Indies'. A series of knavish manoeuvres resulted in the abdication of King Carlos IV and pushing aside his son Fernando, the Prince of the Asturias, in order to make way for Joseph. A Napoleonic administration, it was reasoned, would bring progress and reorganize Spain so that it would become a modern nation. However, French political propaganda was soon checked by some hard realities. Some French troops in Spain, from generals to privates, showed little respect for their Spanish allies, some going so far as to stable their horses in churches. Ordinary Spaniards were increasingly displeased by the callous behaviour of the French troops so that resentment grew as the months passed. If anything, the situation was even worse for the Portuguese where French troops maintained a repressive reign of terror.

LEFT
Napoleon I, Emperor of the French, 1809. This portrait, painted in 1809 by Robert Lefèvre shows the appearance of the Emperor at that time. He was leading the main part of the French army into Austria when the Talavera campaign occurred in Spain. He is shown wearing his usual uniform, the undress jacket of the Imperial Guard's Chasseurs à cheval. (Musée Carnavalet, Paris. Author's photo)

RIGHT
Fernando VII King of Spain. Detained in France by Napoleon since 1808, he remained 'The Desired One' in Spain. He was liberated in 1814 and then came back to Madrid where Francisco Goya made this portrait of the king. He wears the uniform of a captain-general. (Museo del Prado, Madrid. Author's photo)

The arrival of the Portuguese royal family at Rio de Janeiro, Brazil, on 22 January 1808. The extraordinary decision of Prince Regent Joao VI to move with his whole court to Brazil, rather than submit to Napoleon's invading troops, kept Portugal in the war and paved the way for future British interventions in the Peninsula. The arrival of the prince, on board the *Principe Real* (at centre) of 90 guns, accompanied by 15,000 people also signalled the passage from colony to nation, and the birth of independent Brazil, 14 years later, a transition peacefully achieved unlike the regrettable and bloody wars of independence against Spain that engulfed other Latin American nations. (Museu Naval e Oceanografico, Rio de Janeiro. Author's photo)

By 2 May 1808, the population of Madrid had had enough and rose in revolt against the French troops in the city. Led by Marshal Murat, the French repression was quite ferocious with hundreds of badly armed Spaniards slain in the fighting and the prisoners executed by French firing squads the next day. Far from cowing the people, the 'Dos de Mayo' (2 May) became the rallying cry of uprisings that started to break out elsewhere. Soon, all of Spain was in turmoil as the revolt became general. By early June, the news of the uprisings reached northern Portugal. On 6 June, patriotic Portuguese in Porto rose in revolt and were joined by the 6,000 Spanish occupation troops who now turned on their French allies, who instantly became the enemy. A week later, the revolt had swept northern Portugal and, as in Spain, the whole country had raised the standard of revolt. In many parts of Spain, 'juntas' (or, roughly translated, popular assemblies) rose spontaneously to govern in the name of the exiled King Fernando VII. In Portugal, the institutions abolished by the French were restored and the regular and militia regiments were revived. Because the legitimate rulers had simply moved to Brazil, the organization of the country and its armed forces was much more orderly in Portugal than in Spain.

Meanwhile, Napoleon had beckoned his brother Joseph to leave his kingdom in Naples and travel to Madrid to sit on the Spanish throne. He arrived at Bayonne to meet the Spanish officials that supported the new imperial regime, proceeded to Spain and made his formal entry in Madrid on 20 July 1808 with a sizeable escort. The news that French troops had meanwhile looted the churches in the town of Cuenca provoked Spanish outrage everywhere. On 24 July, Joseph wrote to Napoleon that his enemy was 'a nation of 12 million people, brave and totally exasperated. My assassination is publicly spoken about … everything that has been done here [by the French troops] is odious' showing that the people's hatred for him and anything French had become a passion.

Spanish patriots entering Madrid – or the Grand Duke of Berg's Retreat Discovered, 1808. This satiric print after George Cruikshank makes fun of Marshal Murat's predicament in Madrid as the Spanish uprising spread. Here, Murat, who had the title of Duke of Berg, is in an outhouse when Spanish patriots approach. (Anne S.K. Brown Military Collection, Brown University Library, Providence)

The surrender of Gen. Dupont and his army at Bailen, 16 July 1808. On the left, Dupont surrenders his sword while on the right, a Spanish infantryman restrains a French grenadier who is damning his general for this defeat. Watercolour by Maurice Orange done in 1895. (Anne S.K. Brown Military Collection, Brown University Library, Providence. Author's photo)

On 28 July, all of Joseph's efforts to conciliate the parties were swept away as the extraordinary news of Gen. Dupont's defeat and surrender at Bailen on the 19th arrived in Madrid. This was a disastrous event for Joseph and for Napoleon; for the first time, a whole army corps of the 'invincible' French army had laid down its arms. This news spread like wildfire all over Europe. On 31 July, Joseph left Madrid.

French invasion and the retreat from northern Portugal, March–May 1809

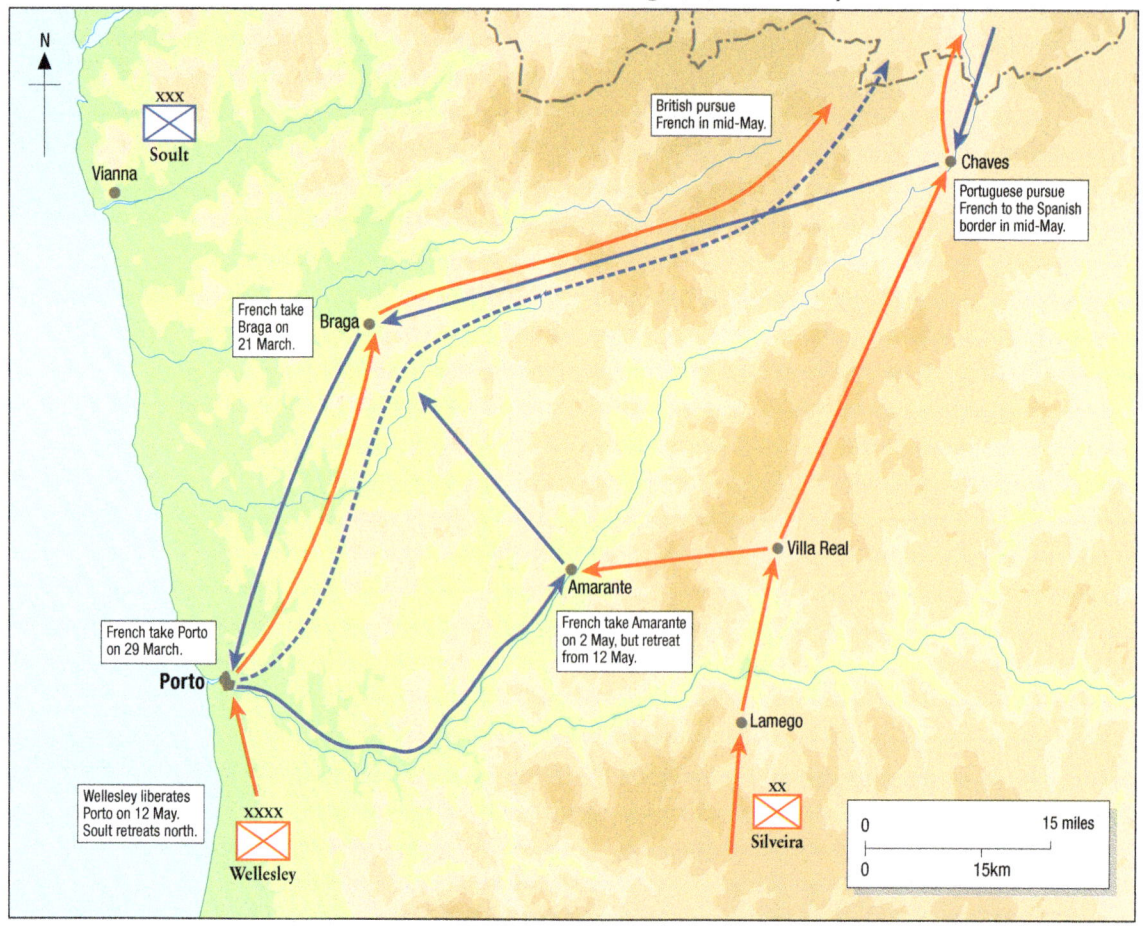

Great Britain was meanwhile assailed with demands for help and rushed an expeditionary force of 8,700 men from England under Lt. Gen. Sir Arthur Wellesley, later to become the Duke of Wellington, which landed on 1 August 1808 at Figueira da Foz in Portugal and was joined by another 5,400-man British contingent from Gibraltar. On 17 August, Wellesley attacked the French at Roliça and soon routed Gen. Delaborde's troops. On 21 August, Wellesley decisively defeated Junot at Vimeiro. After the battle, Wellesley was superseded (because of seniority) by Sir Hew Dalrymple who proceeded to sign the convention of Cintra that allowed the French army to evacuate Portugal. The British now had a solid strategic base on the continent and sent more troops.

Napoleon could not tolerate defeat in Spain and Portugal. He already had diplomatic difficulties elsewhere with, notably, Austria, and felt that this would eventually lead to hostilities in the following spring. Therefore, the Iberian problem that now sprang up had to be settled at once. French troops in Spain were regrouping at Vittoria under the leadership of King Joseph and Marshal Jourdan. On 5 November 1808, Napoleon arrived there at the head of some 200,000 men putting the total of his army in Spain at about 300,000 troops. On 2 December, Napoleon was in sight of Madrid with his huge army and the city surrendered; on 19 December, Barcelona fell. The resistance of the Spanish armies was gradually collapsing in the face of Napoleon's tremendous onslaught.

His Royal Highness the Prince of Wales at a review, 1809. Because of King George III's lapses into mental illness, the Prince of Wales would occasionally be called upon to be the de facto head of state of Great Britain, a situation formally recognized when he was named Prince Regent in February 1811. This very large portrait by John Singleton Copley, said to have been painted in 1809, the year of Talavera, shows the prince wearing the uniform of a field marshal although this is a rank that he never actually achieved as an officer. He is attended by Lord Heathfield, Gen. Turner and Baron Eben; Col. Quinton is in the distance. Of these, Baron Eben, a Prussian officer who was ADC to the prince, was then serving in Portugal as lieutenant-colonel of the Loyal Lusitanian Legion so some aspects of the painting would have been done earlier. It was also retouched later, as shown by the prince's gold *aiguillette*, introduced for generals' uniforms in July 1811, traces of his over-painted epaulettes are still visible. Lord Heathfield's general's uniform was not altered. (Boston Museum of Fine Art. Author's photo)

In late November 1808, Maj. Gen. Sir John Moore at the head of some 25,000 British troops entered Spain and threatened Marshal Soult's 2nd Corps. Napoleon sent Marshal Ney's 6th Corps ahead to the rescue and he himself followed with his Imperial Guard. Sir John Moore perceived the danger of being trapped by Soult's and Ney's corps and headed for Corunna, the main port in north-western Spain, where his army could be evacuated on British ships. On 16 January 1809, the French attacked Moore's army, but did not succeed in breaking the British defence position at Corunna although Sir John Moore was killed in the fighting. Two days later, the last British troops embarked and were on their way to England. Meanwhile, on 1 January 1809, Napoleon had received urgent news regarding worsening relations with Austria and Russia. He turned back near Astorga and headed for Paris. Major-General Sir John Cradock replaced Moore in Portugal to command the 20,000 British troops there. All he seemed to think about was getting his army, which he regrouped in Lisbon, out of Portugal.

Portuguese levies and the new, British-trained, Loyal Lusitanian Legion led by Sir Robert Wilson were all that stood to defend northern Portugal against Marshal Soult's veteran troops. As it was, Sir Robert sent his legionnaires on a series of daring raids into the Spanish plains of Leon during the winter and spring of 1809, some going as far as Avila, which greatly upset the French who thought they were facing a mixed Anglo-Portuguese army instead of a few hundred men (see *Oldest Allies: Alcantara 1809* in Osprey's Raid series). Further into western Spain above Portugal, Marshal Soult opted to invade northern Portugal. His 22,000 men crossed the border, Portuguese defences crumbled and, on 29 March 1809, Soult's troops took the city of Porto amidst considerable slaughter.

This time, substantial British help was on the way. On 22 April 1809, Lt. Gen. Sir Arthur Wellesley landed at Lisbon to replace Gen. Cradock. The British cabinet had correctly sensed that Cradock's view of the military situation in the Peninsula was too pessimistic. Wellesley's priority was to clear the French out of northern Portugal. At the head of a 46,000-man Anglo-Portuguese army, Wellesley liberated Porto on 12 May 1809 and pursued the French up to the border. With the French out of northern Portugal, Wellesley now mooted an advance into Spain.

CHRONOLOGY

1807

27 October — Treaty of Fontainebleau between France and Spain; its secret clauses provide for the invasion and breaking up of Portugal into three parts.

19 November — General Junot's French troops start crossing into Portugal.

27–29 November — Prince Regent Joao VI and the court sail from Lisbon towards Brazil. The next day, Junot enters Lisbon with French troops.

1808

2 May — Insurrection against the French in Madrid, bloodily repressed in the city, but revolt spreads throughout Spain.

10 May — Napoleon names his brother Joseph as King of Spain; the Spanish want Fernando VII as king and the nation rallies around his name.

6 June — Northern and central Portugal rises against the French; revolt spreads throughout the country.

19 July — Defeat and surrender of Gen. Dupont's French army at Bailen to Gen. Castanos's Spanish army.

31 July — King Joseph and French troops evacuate Madrid.

September — After being defeated at Roliça and Vimeiro by Lt. Gen. Sir Arthur Wellesley, Junot and the French army evacuate Portugal.

November — Napoleon enters Spain at the head of 300,000 men to restore French domination and takes Madrid.

1809

16 January — Major-General Sir John Moore killed at the battle of Corunna but his British army is safely evacuated.

6 April — Lieutenant-General Sir Arthur Wellesley appointed to command in Portugal as commander-in-chief of the British and Portuguese forces. Arrives in Lisbon on 22 April.

12 May	Porto taken from Marshal Soult's French forces who retreat north into Galicia (Spain).
25 June	Marshal Victor's 1st Corps withdrawing from Estramadura reaches Talavera, leaves a rearguard there and proceeds to Cazalegas further east.
27 June	Wellesley's army marches from Abrantes (Portugal) and crosses the border into Estramadura (Spain) in early July.
10–11 July	First meeting between Lt. Gen. Wellesley and Gen. Cuesta at Casa de Miravete near Almaraz.
21 July	Lieutenant-General Wellesley's British army makes its junction with Gen. Cuesta's Spanish force at Oropesa. At noon on the outskirts, a Spanish cavalry patrol clashes with a French light cavalry patrol that is driven off. But a large French dragoon force arrives and is met by a large body of Spanish cavalry. The French hold their ground and retreat only when British cavalry reinforcements arrive.
22 July	Marshal Jourdan and King Joseph in Madrid learn of the Anglo-Spanish army's junction and advance; Sébastiani's 4th Corps is ordered to join Victor's army; on 24 July, Jourdan and King Joseph also go to join Victor with further reinforcements from the Madrid Garrison.
27–28 July	Battle of Talavera.
29 July	Marshal Soult's 2nd Corps is marching south through Estramadura; he is followed by Marshal Ney's and Mortier's corps.
3 August	Lieutenant-General Wellesley learns of French corps to his west flank and decides to evacuate Talavera.
4 August	Last and bitter meeting between generals Wellesley and Cuesta at Oropesa. British army leaves Talavera, eventually followed by Spanish.
8 August	General Cuesta's Spanish army defeated by Marshal Mortier's 5th French Corps and Marshal Soult's 2nd Corps at Puente del Arzobispo.
8 August	King Joseph and Sébastiani's 4th French Corps defeat Spanish army under Gen. Venegas at Almonacid south of Toledo.
12 August	Sir Robert Wilson's detachment scattered by Marshal Ney at Baños.
3 September	Lieutenant-General Wellesley establishes the HQ of his army at Badajos until 25 December.
16 September	Following his appointment as viscount, Lt. Gen. Wellesley henceforth signs his name as 'Wellington'.

OPPOSING COMMANDERS

THE BRITISH

Lieutenant-General Sir Arthur Wellesley, Viscount Wellington (1769–1852). The future Duke of Wellington was born in Ireland and joined the army in 1787. He campaigned in Holland during 1794–95, then in India from 1796 where he won much distinction for his victories over the Marathas at Assaye and Argaun in 1803. Back in England in 1806, opportunities for commands were relatively few although he led a brigade at Copenhagen in 1807. Gazetted lieutenant-general, he was put in command of the troops sailing to Portugal in July 1808 where he performed brilliantly during August. However, Sir Harry Burrard and Sir Hew Dalrymple were senior to Wellesley and he was superseded the day he won the battle of Vimeiro over Gen. Junot. Wellesley was again put in charge of the British forces in Portugal in April 1809 and retook Porto from Marshal Soult's French troops who went back into Spain. The summer found him making a foray into Spain as far as Talavera. He was thereafter raised to the peerage and titled Wellington. In 1810, he repelled the final French invasion of Portugal, then fought in Spain and was ultimately in southern France by 1814. He is of course most famous for his victory over Napoleon at Waterloo on 18 June 1815. This extraordinary man went on to be commander-in-chief of the army and prime minister.

John Coape Sherbrooke (1764–1830) entered the army in 1780 and served in the 33rd Foot in North America, the Low Countries and, from 1796, India where he was present at the siege of Seringapatam. While in India, he developed persistent health problems and came back to England. In 1805, he was promoted to major-general and sent to Sicily where, besides commanding the Sicilian Regiment, he mostly acted as a diplomat. He was renowned as 'an officer, full of energy, rousing others to exertion, and indefatigable in his own person' according to his comrade Henry Edward Bunbury. He arrived in the Peninsula in 1809 with the local rank of lieutenant-general and second in command to Sir Arthur Wellesley, whom he knew from his younger days in the 33rd Foot. He distinguished himself at Porto and Talavera and was made Knight Commander of Bath in September 1809. Health problems plagued him and, in 1810, he returned to England to recuperate. In 1811, he was named governor of Nova Scotia and, in 1816, governor general of British North America at Quebec until 1818 when his failing health dictated his retirement and return to England.

Rowland Hill (1772–1842) was commissioned in 1790 and campaigned at Toulon and in Egypt. A major-general by 1808, he commanded one of the brigades in the army in Portugal with efficiency and good judgement and served with distinction under Sir John Moore in the Corunna campaign. When Wellesley once again assumed command of the British and Portuguese forces in 1809, Hill was with him at the retaking of Porto and throughout the Talavera campaign, during which he commanded the 2nd British Brigade. Wellesley often entrusted Hill with independent commands as he had the uncanny ability almost to emulate his commander's thinking. He was well known in the army for his kindness to the men and he was consequently quite popular. He later became ill with malaria, was successfully treated in Britain and was back in Portugal in May 1811. During the remainder of the Peninsular War, Hill was always Wellington's most trusted independent corps commander. He also was present at the battle of Waterloo in 1815. From 1828 to 1839, he succeeded the Duke of Wellington as commander-in-chief of the Forces.

Lieutenant-General Sir John Coape Sherbrooke, c. 1810. He was in command of the 1st British Division at Talavera. He was also present at the previous battle of Porto and was knighted in September 1809 for his services. Poor health forced him to go back to England the following year. He wears the full dress uniform of his rank, a scarlet coat with blue facings, gold epaulettes, gold buttons and embroidered buttonholes. Print after portrait. (Private collection. Author's photo)

THE SPANISH

Captain-General Gregorio Garcia de La Cuesta y Fernandez de Celis (1741–1811). Born in Cantabria, Cuesta entered the Toledo Regiment in 1758, served in America during the 1780s and, by 1793, had risen to brigadier-general. He distinguished himself in late 1793, forcing the French to evacuate Roussillon towns including Collioure during the short First Coalition War. In March 1808, he was promoted to Captain-General of Old Castilla and, a short time later, appointed to be Viceroy of New Spain (Mexico). However, the outbreak of revolts against the French in May kept him in Spain and he chose to fight for the restoration of King Fernando VII rather than join Joseph Bonaparte's new Napoleonic government. Cuesta initially had only a few thousand men that were easily driven off by the French, so he combined his forces with those of Lt. Gen. Joaquim Blake, but they were defeated at Medina del Rio Seco on 14 July 1808. Always active in political intrigues, a necessary skill for Spanish generals at this time, he was arrested and briefly detained, before being tasked with the organization and command of the Army of Estramadura. He quickly achieved this in spite of lacking all sorts of promised but undelivered supplies and, in early 1809, drove the French out of the province of Badajos. The French counter-attacked in March and, at Medellin, he was defeated and wounded during the battle when ridden over by cavalry. He survived but the consequences were painful and he thereafter travelled in a carriage lying on pillows whenever he could. His army then joined Wellesley for the Talavera campaign. Later, Cuesta suffered defeats, to the delight of his political enemies, and he resigned in November 1810, retiring at Majorca where he died from the consequences of his wounds. Cuesta was a fiercely proud, very brave and stubborn officer who was often condemned by British observers as being extremely difficult to collaborate with. It should also be noted that he was a devoted leader of an army that lacked almost everything during some of the most desperate times in Spain's long history.

General Juan O'Donoju (1762–1821). Born in Sevilla of Irish descent, he entered the Spanish army and rose to field rank. In 1808, he fought the French in Aragon and was later attached to Gen. Cuesta's Army of Estramadura. He was a diplomatic individual and fluent in English, assets that proved very important for communications with senior British officers during the Talavera campaign, especially in view of Gen. Cuesta's intransigent attitude. Following the Peninsular War, O'Donoju became a minister in the government, captain-general and, in 1821, was appointed viceroy of Mexico. He arrived in the country in July, perceived that its independence movement was unstoppable and negotiated a fairly peaceful transition that prevented much bloodshed. He became ill and died in Mexico City in November.

Captain-General Gregorio de La Cuesta, commander of the Spanish army at Talavera. This unsigned profile likeness print appears to date from the early or middle 1790s, notably because the general's coat has a stand-and-fall collar as well as showing a somewhat younger man. He was 68 at the time of the battle. (Private collection. Author's photo)

THE FRENCH

Marshal Victor, Duke of Belluno (1764–1841). Claude-Victor Perrin, called simply Victor, entered the artillery as a private at age 17, was noticed by Col. Bonaparte at the 1793 siege of Toulon for his leadership qualities and rose to the rank of division general in 1797. His talents proved quite important when leading the left of the French army at Marengo in 1800. American readers may be interested to know that, three years later, he was put in charge of the French troops that were to garrison Louisiana, but the expedition was cancelled when this immense territory was sold to the United States and Victor remained in Europe. He was later present in several battles against the Prussians, notably at Jena in 1806, and won the rank of marshal for his distinguished conduct at Friedland the following year. He was also ambassador to Prussia and was rewarded with the title of Duke of Belluno in September 1808. He probably liked soldiering better than diplomacy and was called to Spain where his opponents respected his military skills. At Talavera, he proved to be the most aggressive of the French field officers with a quick, tactical eye that immediately found the flaw in the British position. In 1812, he commanded a corps in Russia and played a distinguished part in the retreating French army's crossing of the Berezina River and took part in the 1813 campaign. In February 1814, he was violently blamed and suspended by Napoleon for bringing his troops late at Montereau-sur-Yonne, which deeply hurt his pride. He transferred his allegiance to Louis XVIII's royal government and continued to be active in the army after 1815, notably as minister of war (1821–23). He retired in 1830.

Marshal Victor, commander of the 1st French Army Corps. Claude-Victor Perrin was known as Victor. He became marshal in 1807 and Duke of Bellune the following year. Unsigned portrait of c.1826. (Musée de l'Armée, Paris. Author's photo)

LEFT
Marshal Jean-Baptiste Jourdan, chief of staff to King Joseph of Spain. He was the senior French marshal in Spain at the time of the Talavera campaign. (Musée de l'Armée, Paris. Author's photo)

CENTRE
General Horace Sébastiani, commander of 4th French Army Corps. Contemporary print. (Anne S.K. Brown Military Collection, Brown University Library, Providence. Author's photo)

RIGHT
General of Division Jean-Joseph Dessolle, c.1800. In 1809, Dessolle's division was the main French force in Madrid. Part of it was sent to join the army which fought at Talavera. (Musée de l'Armée, Paris. Author's photo)

Marshal Jean-Baptiste Jourdan (1762–1833) joined the Auxerrois Regiment as a private soldier in 1778 and was present at the abortive siege of Savannah (USA) in September 1779. He returned to France in 1782 and left the army owing to health problems incurred in the West Indies. In 1789, he joined the French Revolution's National Guard and, from 1791, went on active service, quickly becoming a general of division by 1793. He brilliantly took part in several campaigns in western Germany from 1794 to 1799, but was somewhat disgraced by his retreat against superior forces as well as his association with Gen. Moreau, Napoleon's political rival. Recognizing Jourdan's military as well as his political and diplomatic abilities, Napoleon appointed him ambassador and, in 1804, promoted him to the rank of marshal. In 1806, he was attached to Joseph Bonaparte as his senior military adviser as king of Naples, a task he continued in Spain two years later when Joseph became king of Spain. Disgraced following the battle of Talavera, Jourdan retired in France, but Napoleon called him back to duty in 1811 as chief of staff in Spain. However, Madrid had to be evacuated in 1812 and, the following year, with King Joseph, he suffered a decisive defeat at Vittoria where his marshal's baton was captured, although he got away safely. He held no important commands thereafter.

King Joseph Bonaparte (1768–1844), also named King Joseph-Napoleon in Spain. He was Emperor Napoleon's elder brother and a lawyer who entered politics in the 1790s and, as his brother rose to power, also became a noted diplomat being instrumental in concluding treaties with the USA, Austria and Great Britain between 1800 and 1802. Generally recognized as Emperor Napoleon's most able brother, he was named King of Naples in 1806 and King of Spain two years later. But nearly all Spaniards abhorred him as a French puppet and he indeed had few if any powers over the French marshals in Spain. Because his early legislation in Spain concerned the repression of gambling and heavy drinking, as well as a persistent rumour that he liked to drink, witty Spaniards nicknamed him 'Pepe la Botella' (Pepe the bottle) in derision and the name stuck to him in all classes of Spanish society. He was forced to flee to France in 1813 and abdicated the throne of Spain. After Napoleon's fall, he went to the United States and lived mostly at his estate of Point Breeze, New Jersey, between 1817 and 1832. He thereafter returned to Europe and passed away in Florence, Italy.

OPPOSING FORCES

THE BRITISH

The great majority of the army consisted of infantry and most of that was line infantry. By 1809, most of the 103 regiments of the line had two battalions, one only usually being deployed in a theatre of operation. The strength of a British regiment could vary greatly and these differences were not only due to a lack of recruits and losses in the field, but also to the numbers of their authorized 'establishment' as voted by Parliament. Hence the considerable differences in numbers one routinely sees in British army listings. The 'British' army in Spain included a sizeable number of Germans, mostly Hanoverians in the King's German Legion, who served with distinction. The British army's organization was not then as sophisticated as the French in that there were no corps. Lieutenant-General Wellesley's army at Talavera was thus divided into divisions.

British line infantrymen carried the India Pattern musket with its socket bayonet. This was a very sturdy, not too fancy weapon, which fired a .75-cal. bullet. The 60th and 95th Rifles were armed with rifles, a very precise

LEFT
Officer, 3rd Dragoon Guards, c.1800–1811. This regiment was part of Henry Fane's Cavalry Brigade at Talavera. The uniform shown was worn until 1811. Watercolour by S. Harding. (Anne S.K. Brown Military Collection, Brown University Library, Providence. Author's photo)

RIGHT
Sergeant, British line infantry, c.1806–1811. Watercolour by R. Wymer. (Anne S.K. Brown Military Collection, Brown University Library, Providence. Author's photo)

LEFT
Private of 60th Foot's 5th (Rifles) Battalion priming his rifle, c.1808–1815. Five companies of these units were individually detached to five brigades and the other five companies formed part of Donkin's 2nd Brigade in the British 3rd Division. Thus, parties of these 'green jackets' were spread as skirmishers with most of the British force. Print after P.W. Reynolds. (Private collection. Author's photo)

RIGHT
Officer, Royal Artillery, c.1805. This was the uniform worn by artillery officers until 1812. The individual pictured is Capt. George W. Unett who became brevet major in 1814 and was present at Waterloo. Watercolour by Denis Dighton. (Anne S.K. Brown Military Collection, Brown University Library, Providence. Author's photo)

weapon for skirmishers. The uniform was red except for the rifle units whose men wore dark green. The men wore black felt cylindrical shakos with brass plates in front. White breeches and black knee gaiters were the official dress but, in the Peninsula, the infantry was usually seen in comfortable white linen pantaloons. British dragoons wore red coatees and bicorn hats while light dragoons had dark blue dolmans and leather 'Tarleton' helmets with bearskin crests. The straight-bladed Model 1796 heavy cavalry sword used by dragoons was considered one of the worst weapons of its day while the curved-bladed 1796 light cavalry sword was appreciated as one of the best. There were problems in finding suitable horses in the Peninsula and British cavalry was considered as fair, but not as seasoned as its opponent.

British soldiers were not above stealing and, in a few cases, murdering helpless civilians. They would be executed if caught. The standard of discipline was one of the harshest in any European army with even minor offences punished by floggings with a 'cat-o'-nine-tails'. For all that, offences were frequent, especially for getting drunk. British infantrymen drilled according to the practical 1788 '19 steps' by Sir David Dundas. Drill was most rigorous and British soldiers, even when their line was formed of only two ranks, could fire some of Europe's most murderous volleys three times a minute. Such firepower was matched by precise manoeuvres and considerable coolness in battle. As a result, although the British army was usually smaller than its opponents, it was one of the most lethal forces in Europe when it came to firepower and steadiness in combat. The officers were generally talented and educated men who had their men's respect. On the whole, the fighting spirit of the army was excellent.

For the Talavera campaign, Wellesley reorganized his forces while at Abrantes in mid-June. The infantry was divided into four divisions that were to be relatively autonomous from one another. Divisions usually had two brigades, but, at Talavera, Sherbrooke's 1st Division had four, the two extra being made up of the King's German Legion. Wellesley had appreciated in previous battles the redoubtable efficiency of the screens of French *voltigeurs* deployed ahead of their line regiments. He therefore attached permanently to each brigade companies of riflemen from 5th Battalion of the 60th Regiment. They were armed with Baker rifles that were much slower to load, but far more accurate than ordinary muskets, and used to 'pick off' French *voltigeurs* from a distance. Added to the light companies from each battalion, the brigades thus had a sizeable portion of light infantry to cope with the enemy's *voltigeurs*. The cavalry division was also divided into three brigades, one of heavy and two of light cavalry regiments.

THE SPANISH

The pre-1808 Spanish Army was organized much like other western-European armies of the later 18th century, the French Army having been its main model. There was a general staff led by captain-generals, the equivalent of field marshal, and a sizeable administrative body of staff officers. The regular troops were assisted by battalions of provincial militia and companies of urban militia. In 1808, the army on service amounted to about 7,000 officers and 130,000 NCOs and enlisted men, including 30,000 mobilized militiamen. Mounted regiments had five squadrons of two companies each. Line infantry regiments had three battalions of four companies each including two grenadier companies per regiment. Light infantry battalions had six companies. The artillery had four regiments in 1808 and was considered an elite corps as were the engineers.

Following the 2 May 1808 uprising, the regular army's organization collapsed while new units spontaneously appeared all over Spain. In occupied areas, many men took to the hills and became what would be known as guerrillas. By the end of 1808, various local 'junta' governments appeared and a Central Junta was also set up in Sevilla. As can be seen by the order of battle of Gen. Cuesta's army, the Spanish forces were now a mixture of pre-1808 regiments and new units that bore such names as 'Leales de Fernando VII' or 'Tiradores de Merida'. Older infantry units

LEFT TO RIGHT

Standard-bearer and trooper of the Spanish Infante Cavalry Regiment, c.1807. This regiment was in the 2nd Cavalry Division under the command of the Duke of Albuquerque at Talavera. Print after C. Shur. (Anne S.K. Brown Military Collection, Brown University Library, Providence. Author's photo)

Officer of the Irlanda Regiment, c.1809–1811. Two battalions of this unit were part of Maj. Gen. R. Manglano's 4th Infantry Division. Print after Goddard and Booth. (Canadian War Museum, Ottawa. Author's photo)

Spanish infantry, 1809. The Spanish troops at the time of the Talavera campaign lacked arms, uniforms and equipment. The luckier infantrymen might still have their pre-1808 white uniforms as seen in this 1809 print after J. Booth. Private collection. (Author's photo)

Canarias Infantry Battalion, 1810. This battalion, which was part of the regular garrison of the Canary Islands, arrived in Cadiz in April 1809 and attached to Gen. Cuesta's Army of Andalusia. It was part of 1st Infantry Division led by the Marques de Zayas at Talavera. Watercolour by Antonio Pacheco. (Collection and photo: Biblioteca Publica Municipal, Santa Cruz de Tenerife, Canary Islands)

mostly had their white uniforms, but many new units had dark blue uniforms, which, at times, could be confused for those of French troops; light cavalry was mostly dressed in blue or green, heavy cavalry in dark blue and dragoons in yellow. Although the British and Portuguese were now their allies, the Spanish – generals in particular – had deep suspicions about them; they had been the traditional enemies of Spain since the Middle Ages. Regimental officers were not considered to have, in general, particularly remarkably good knowledge of military affairs by both their British and French counterparts who also felt they often were rather vain. The enlisted men were seen as good and capable of great courage as well as sudden panic when they were indifferently led.

The efficiency of the Spanish army, which had been very good in the reign of King Carlos III (1759–88), had considerably declined under King Carlos IV (1788–1808) and practically collapsed in 1808. Suffice it to say here that while Spanish soldiers could be very brave in hand-to-hand combat, they often were woefully inefficient in the linear tactics, as used in battles at that time. Their manoeuvres and drill left a lot to be desired compared with their allies and their enemies. Much worse, their firepower was usually reckoned at two shots per minute, instead of three shots a minute achieved by their French opponents and their British allies. The older Spanish weapons were generally good and, in the case of muskets, of the same calibre as the French.

THE FRENCH

From 18 February 1808, each regiment of French line infantry was to have five battalions, four on service and one acting as the regimental depot. Each service battalion had a company of grenadiers, one of *voltigeurs* – light infantry skirmishers – and four of fusiliers, all companies to have 140 men including three officers. With battalion staff, eagle-bearers and musicians, the regimental establishment totalled 3,908 men including 78 officers. The actual strength of the regiments in the field was often much less, as can be seen in the order of battle. In Spain, the regiments usually had three service battalions. The light infantry *chasseurs* had the same establishment except that their grenadiers

LEFT TO RIGHT
Trooper of the French 2nd Hussars Regiment, c.1807. This unit was part of 1st Corps' cavalry. Otto manuscript. (Anne S.K. Brown Military Collection, Brown University Library, Providence. Author's photo)

Trooper, 2nd French Dragoons, c.1809. Dressed in marching order as part of this regiment and served as infantry on foot. It was one of Gen. Latour-Maubourg's cavalry reserve units. Watercolour by Pierre Albert Leroux. (Anne S.K. Brown Military Collection, Brown University Library, Providence. Author's photo)

Trooper, elite company, French Dragoons, c.1808–1813. The scarlet collar and cuffs could correspond to 1st, 3rd, 4th and 6th regiments. The 1st and 4th were at Talavera. Watercolour by Charlet. (Anne S.K. Brown Military Collection, Brown University Library, Providence. Author's photo)

LEFT
French foot artillery officer, c.1809–1811. This print from Goddard and Booth's *Military Costume of Europe* published in 1812 shows a number of figures from Marshal Victor's 1st Army Corps that must have been sent to the London publisher by a British observer in Spain. (Canadian War Museum, Ottawa. Author's photo)

CENTRE
Private of *voltigeurs*, Frankfurt Infantry Battalion, 1809. This German unit was part of General Leval's 2nd Division. Watercolour by Pierre Albert Leroux. (Anne S.K. Brown Military Collection, Brown University Library, Providence. Author's photo)

RIGHT
French Line Infantry, summer campaign dress, Spain, c.1809. White linen shako covers and loose white trousers were often used and those items are shown in the sketches of French troops attributed to one 'El Guil' in Spain. Watercolour by Pierre Albert Leroux. (Anne S.K. Brown Military Collection, Brown University Library, Providence. Author's photo)

were termed *carabiniers* although they were armed with ordinary muskets rather than rifles (*carabine* in French). The standard French infantry musket was the sturdy 1777 or Year IX model that was .69-cal. French cavalry regiments usually had five squadrons, each having two companies, but these were often dispersed in different armies. The sabres of both the light and the medium cavalry were generally rated amongst the best such weapons anywhere. The artillery was considered one of Europe's finest and served the dependable Gribeauval system guns. In 1809, infantrymen wore dark blue uniforms as did gunners. Dragoons had brass helmets and dark green coats, *chasseurs à cheval* had shakos and dark green jackets while hussars had braided uniforms of various colours.

An enduring misconception about the French infantry in the Napoleonic wars is that it always attacked in columns while its opponents would be formed in lines – the so-called 'column versus line' tactics. French infantrymen would indeed normally march up in columns. But, as they neared their opponents, would deploy into lines as specified by their 1791 drill. The French infantry lines were formed three ranks deep and were always, in theory, preceded by a screen of light infantry *voltigeurs*. But this was not always followed in the Peninsula. In practice, they often could not deploy in lines from columns owing to the type of terrain Wellesley cleverly chose. Their firepower, which averaged three shots per minute, while correct for a modern army was inferior to the exceptionally steady and murderous volleys of British (and later Portuguese) troops. The French were, however, very fearsome in bayonet attacks. The French cavalry in the Peninsula was generally very dependable and manoeuvred quite competently. It was a well-trained body of troops that usually kept reasonable control in battle. At Talavera, the French army had a sizeable contingent of light cavalry and dragoons, but no heavy cavalry such as *cuirassiers*. Many cavalry units had previously served victoriously in other parts of Europe so they had numbers of experienced campaigners within their ranks.

Napoleon's army deployed in Spain included many units detached from allied European states. At Talavera, these included contingents from smaller German states, King Louis Bonaparte's Kingdom of Holland and Poles from the Grand Duchy of Warsaw, nearly all of whom were in 4th Corps and generally considered to be good troops. Finally, Dessolle's 5,700-man division included 2,100 soldiers from King Joseph's Spanish royal guard, but part of which was recruited from Frenchmen and other nationalities.

ORDERS OF BATTLE

BRITISH ARMY (25 JULY 1809)
Compiled from Oman

Commander-in-chief: Sir Arthur Wellesley
Cavalry Division, William Payne
Henry Fane's Brigade
    3rd Dragoon Guards   525
    4th Dragoons   545
Stapleton Cotton's Brigade
    14th Light Dragoons   464
    16th Light Dragoons   525
George Anson's Brigade
    23rd Light Dragoons   459
    1st Light Dragoons, King's German Legion   451
Total cavalry   2,969

1st Infantry Division, Lt. Gen. John Coape Sherbrooke
1st Brigade (Guards), Brig. Gen. Henry Campbell
    2nd (Coldstream) Guards, 1st Battalion   970
    3rd (Scots) Guards, 1st Battalion   1,019
    60th Foot, 5th (Rifle) Battalion, one company   56
2nd Brigade, Brig. Gen. Alan Cameron
    61st Foot, 1st Battalion   778
    83rd Foot, 2nd Battalion   535
    60th Foot, 5th (Rifle) Battalion, one company   51
3rd Brigade, Brig. Gen. Ernest, Baron Langwerth
    King's German Legion, 1st line battalion   604
    King's German Legion, 2nd line battalion   678
    King's German Legion, light companies   106
4th Brigade, Brig. Gen. Sigismund, Baron Löw
    King's German Legion, 5th line battalion   610
    King's German Legion, 7th line battalion   557
Total 1st Division   5,964

2nd Infantry Division, Maj. Gen. Rowland Hill
1st Brigade, Brig. Gen. Christopher Tilson
    3rd Foot, 1st Battalion   746
    48th Foot, 2nd Battalion   567
    66th Foot, 2nd Battalion   526
    60th Foot, 5th (Rifle) Battalion, one company   64
2nd Brigade, Brig. Gen. Richard Stewart
    29th Foot, 1st Battalion   598
    48th Foot, 1st Battalion   807
    1st Battalion of detachments (mostly from 42nd,
        79th and 92nd Highlanders)   609
Total 2nd Division   3,905

3rd Infantry Division, Maj. Gen. Randoll Mackenzie
1st Brigade, Maj. Gen. Randoll Mackenzie
    24th Foot, 2nd Battalion   787
    31st Foot, 2nd Battalion   733
    45th Foot, 1st Battalion   756
2nd Brigade, Col. Rufane Donkin
    87th Foot, 2nd Battalion   599
    88th Foot, 1st Battalion   599
    60th Foot, 5th (Rifle) Battalion, five companies   273
Total 3rd Division   3,747

4th Infantry Division, Brig. Gen. Alexander Campbell
1st Brigade, Brig. Gen. Alexander Campbell
    7th Foot, 2nd Battalion   431
    53rd Foot, 2nd Battalion   537
    60th Foot, 5th (Rifle) Battalion, one company   56
2nd Brigade, Col. James Kemmis
    40th Foot, 1st Battalion   745
    97th Foot   502
    2nd Battalion of detachments   625
    60th Foot, 5th (Rifle) Battalion, one company   56
Total 4th Division   2,960

Royal Artillery, three batteries
    (Lawson's, Sillery's and Elliot's)   681
King's German Legion Artillery, two batteries
    (Rettberg's and Helse's)   330
Royal Engineers   22
Royal Staff Corps   63

Total British Army   20,641

SPANISH ARMY OF ESTRAMADURA (MID-JULY 1809)

The orders of battle of the Spanish troops are confused, lack detail and are contradictory. We have used Oman's as our main reference with J. J. S. Bayon's for Brig. Gen. Bermuy's Reserve and some divisional additions (shown in square brackets).

Commander-in-chief: Gen. Gregorio de La Cuesta
Second in command: Gen. Francisco de Eguia
Chief of Staff: Gen. Juan O'Donoju

1st Cavalry Division, Lt. Gen. J. de Henestrosa
    El Rey Cavalry
    Calatrava
    Voluntario de Espana
    Imperial de Toledo
    Cazadores de Sevilla
    Reyna Dragoons
    Villaviciosa Dragoons
    Cazadores de Madrid

[Caceres Dragoons, Infante Cavalry, Jerez Lancers, Almanza Dragoons]

2nd Cavalry Division, Lt. Gen. Duke of Albuquerque
    Carabineros Reales (one squadron)
    Infante Cavalry
    Alcantara
    Pavia Dragoons
    Almanza Dragoons
    1st Hussars of Estramadura
    2nd Hussars of Estramadura
    [Toledo Cazadores, Sevilla Cavalry,
      Bourbon Cavalry, Madrid Cazadores]

Total   7,000 cavalry

Vanguard, Brig. Gen. José Zayas
    2nd Voluntarios de Cataluna
    Cazadores de Barbastro (2nd Battalion)
    Cazadores de Campo Mayor
    Cazadores de Valencia y Albuquerque
    Cazadores Voluntarios de Valencia (2nd Battalion)
    [Cazadores de Estramadura. Bayon adds a cavalry component:
      Sevilla Cazadores, Grenada Cazadores, Espana Cazadores,
      Calatrava Cavalry, Villaviciosa Dragoons, Andalusia
      Perseguidores Lancers, one company of horse artillery]

1st Infantry Division, Maj. Gen. Marques de Zayas
    Cantabria (three battalions)
    Grenaderos Provinciales
    Canarias
    Tiradores de Merida
    Provincial de Trujillo
    [Cadix Tiradores, Serena Cazadores, Jaen,
      3rd Castilla grenadiers, Tuy Provincial]

2nd Infantry Division, Maj. Gen. Vincente Iglesias
    2nd Majorca
    Velez-Malaga (three battalions)
    Osuna (two battalions)
    Voluntarios Estrangeros
    Provinciales de Burgos
    [Salamancas Provincial, Toledo Provincial, Sappers]

3rd Infantry Division, Maj. Gen. Marques de Portago
    Badajos (two battalions)
    2nd Cazadores de Antequera
    Imperial de Toledo
    Provincial de Badajos
    Provincial de Guadix
    [1st Trujillo 1st Bn, Osuna Voluntarios]

4th Infantry Division, Maj. Gen. R. Manglano
    Irlanda (2nd and 3rd battalions)
    Jaen (two bns)
    3rd Sevilla
    Leales de Fernando VII (1st Battalion)
    2nd Voluntarios de Madrid
    Voluntarios de la Corona
    [Reding Swiss 2nd Battalion, 1st Trujillo 2nd and 3rd bns]

5th Infantry Division, Maj. Gen. L.A. Bassecourt
    1st Real Marina
    Africa (three battalions)
    Murcia (two battalions)
    Reyna (1st Battalion)
    Provincial de Siguenza

Reserve, Brig. Gen. Juan Bermuy
    Regular grenadiers
    Militia grenadiers
    2nd Real Marina
    Carabinos Reales (cavalry)
    Real Guardias de Corps (cavalry)

Total   about 35,000 infantry and 7,000 cavalry

Artillery, 800 men with 30 guns

At least six infantry battalions (two are specifically known: Merida and 3rd Sevilla) and some cavalry were detached elsewhere and there were about 5,000 men that were sick or on command. The troops present at Talavera are estimated at about 28,000 infantry, 6,000 cavalry and 800 gunners.

Spanish army total   34,800

FRENCH ARMY (15 JULY 1809)

Excluding men sick and detached. Compiled from Oman and Griffon de Pleineville.

Commander-in-chief: King Joseph
Major-General (chief of staff): Marshal Jean-Baptiste Jourdan
Artillery commander: General of Division Alexandre-Antoine
    Huneau de Sénarmont
Engineer commander: General of Division de François-Joseph
    Chaussegros de Léry
Total with 1st Corps Staff   47

1st Army Corps
Marshal Victor, Duc de Bellune
Corps chief of staff: Brig. Gen. Jean-Baptiste-Pierre Semellé

1st Division, Gen. François Amable Ruffin
    9th Light Infantry (three battalions)
    24th Line Regiment (three battalions)
    96th Line Regiment (three battalions)
Total 1st Division   5,286

2nd Division, Gen. Pierre Belon Lapisse
    16th Light Infantry
    8th Line Regiment (three battalions)
    45th Line Regiment (three battalions)
    54th Line Regiment (three battalions)
Total 2nd Division   6,862

3rd Division, Gen. Eugène-Casimir Villatte
    27th Light Infantry
    63rd Line Regiment (three battalions)
    94th Line Regiment (three battalions)
    95th Line Regiment (three battalions)
Total 3rd Division   6,135

1st Corps Cavalry, Gen. Octave Beaumont
    2nd Hussars (three squadrons)
    5th Chasseurs à cheval (three squadrons)
Total 1st Corps Cavalry   980

Total 1st Corps   19,310

4th Army Corps
General of Division Horace Sébastiani
Total with 4th Corps Staff: 13

1st Division, Gen. of Division Horace Sébastiani:
    28th Line Regiment (three battalions)
    32nd Line Regiment (three battalions)
    58th Line Regiment (three battalions)
    75th Line Regiment (three battalions)
Total 1st Division   8,118

2nd (German-Dutch) Division, Gen. of Division Jean-François Leval
    2nd and 4th Dutch regiments (three battalions)
    Nassau Regiment (three battalions)
    Baden Regiment (three battalions)
    Hesse Regiment (three battalions)
    Frankfurth (one battalion)
Total 2nd Division   4,537

Detached from 3rd (Polish) Division at Toledo, Gen. of Division Alexandre Valence
    4th Polish Regiment (two battalions)
Total 3rd (Polish) Division   1,600

4th Corps Cavalry, Gen. Antoine-François-Eugène Merlin
    10th Chasseurs à cheval (three squadrons)
    26th Chasseurs à cheval (two squadrons)
    Vistula Legion (Polish) lancers (four squadrons)
    Westphalian Light Horse (two squadrons)
Total 4th Corps Cavalry   1,188

Total 4th Corps   15,456

Reserve Cavalry
1st Dragoon Division, Gen. of Division Marie-Victor de Fay Latour-Maubourg
    1st Dragoons (two squadrons)
    2nd Dragoons (two squadrons)
    4th Dragoons (two squadrons)
    9th Dragoons (two squadrons)
    14th Dragoons (two squadrons)
    26th Dragoons (two squadrons)
Total 1st Dragoon Division 3,279

2nd Dragoon Division, Gen. of Division Jean-Baptiste Milhaud
    5th Dragoons (two squadrons)
    12th Dragoons (two squadrons)
    16th Dragoons (two squadrons)
    20th Dragoons (two squadrons)
    21st Dragoons (two squadrons)
    3rd Dutch Hussars (four squadrons)
Total 2nd Dragoon Division   2,356

Total Reserve Cavalry   5,635

Brigade from General Division Jean-Joseph Dessolle's Division at Madrid
12th Light (three battalions)
51st Line (three battalions) 3,337 for both regiments.
Royal Guard of King Joseph, infantry, 1st Guard Grenadiers and 1st Guard Voltigeurs, 1,800 for both regiments
Royal Guard of King Joseph, Chevau-Légers Regiment   350
27th Chasseurs à cheval (two squadrons)   250
Total for Brigade   5,737

The French artillery amounted to 66 guns, 36 with 1st Corps and 30 with 4th Corps. Artillerymen included in the divisional totals

Total French army   46,138

OPPOSING PLANS

With Napoleon increasingly preoccupied with mustering forces for the upcoming conflict against Austria, the time seemed right to attempt a bold strike in Spain. This could be done if Lt. Gen. Wellesley's British force united with Gen. Cuesta's Spanish army of Estramadura while Gen. Venegas's Spanish army of La Mancha would march towards Toledo and Madrid. With some good fortune, the French corps would be diverted in various areas, be defeated separately and the Anglo-Spanish forces would then liberate Madrid. The Supreme Junta in Sevilla and the British government approved this grand plan. As plans go, it was very optimistic.

Marshal Nicolas Soult, commander of 2nd French Army Corps. Contemporary print. (Private collection. Author's photo)

On the British side, things went astray right away. Some 15,000 men were sent to Sicily while a large expedition was prepared to land in the Low Countries and, hopefully, take the French naval base of Antwerp (Belgium). Encouraged by the Austrians, who wished such a move to divert some French forces, the planned expedition mustering some 40,000 troops went ahead, but was soon caught up in a political scandal, which involved the sale of officers' commissions by the Duke of York's mistress and caused delays. At the end of July when, at last, the Walcheren expedition did occur, it was an outstanding disaster. One can only wonder what the effect would have been on the Peninsular War if these 55,000 men had been assigned to reinforce Lt. Gen. Wellesley's army instead.

Nevertheless, Lt. Gen. Wellesley wanted to go into Spain where he had been promised sufficient supplies for his army by the Spanish authorities. On 3 July, the 21,000-strong British army under his command crossed into Spain by the difficult mountain trail at Zarza-la-Mayor and went on towards Plasencia. General Cuesta's 34,000 men were moving up into Estramadura to meet Wellesley's army. The grand plan called for the united army to march on Madrid and defeat whatever French

Map of central Spain, c.1810s–1820s. This French map shows the general area with Madrid, the prime objective, at centre right. In July 1809, Marshal Mortier's corps was in the Salamanca and Avila area (top) and marched down to join Marshal Ney's and Soult's corps (upper left) in order to cut off General Wellesley's and Cuesta's combined forces moving towards Talavera de la Reyna (lower centre). They would be met by Marshal Victor's corps, east of Talavera, and Gen. Sébastiani would join him from Toledo. Print after Hugo's *France Militaire*. (Private collection. Author's photo)

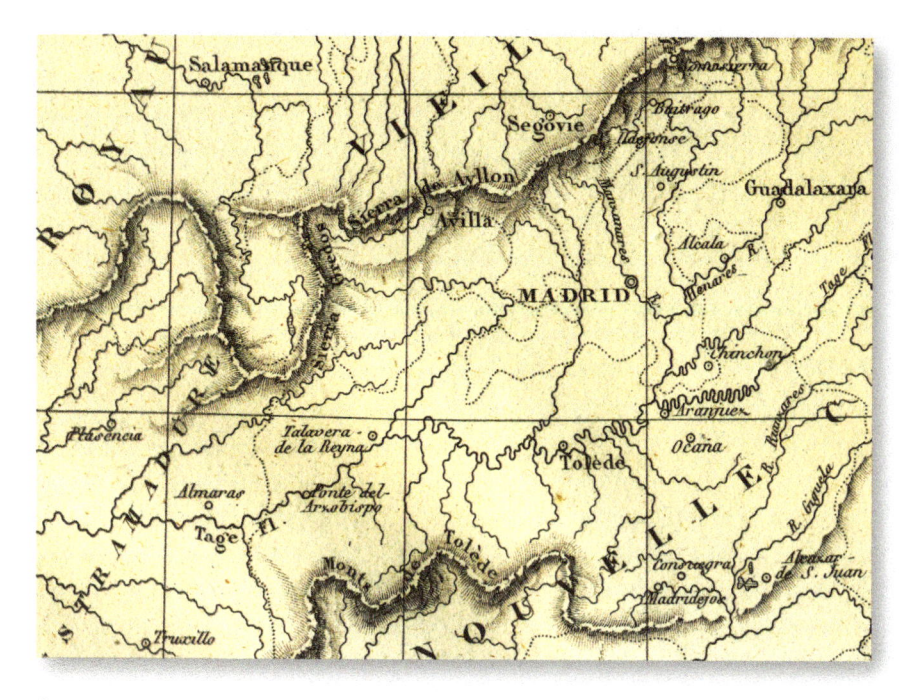

forces would be in the way. At that point the main opponents were likely to be Marshal Victor's 1st Corps, Gen. Sébastiani's 4th Corps at Toledo and, eventually, Madrid's French garrison under King Joseph. General Venegas was to move up his Spanish army of La Mancha towards Toledo and Madrid in order to keep 4th Corps occupied. Thus, there was hope that the 55,000-man Anglo-Spanish army led by generals Wellesley and Cuesta would separately defeat each of the much weaker French corps.

General Antoine-François-Eugène Merlin, c.1810. He commanded the cavalry division attached to the French 4th Corps. On 28 July at Talavera, his division crushed the British cavalry's desperate attempt to outflank the Northern Sector. Print after portrait, private collection. (Author's photo)

THE FRENCH

Naturally, Napoleon's experienced marshals did not take the bait. Appraised that the British and the Spanish were approaching, Marshal Victor and his 1st Corps evacuated Merida and marched towards Talavera de la Reyna. In Madrid, Marshal Jourdan, the senior marshal in Spain, and King Joseph were reorganizing the disposition of the troops they had. The 4th Corps would be ready to leave a minimal garrison in Toledo and join 1st Corps at Talavera.

Now that Marshal Soult's 2nd Corps had evacuated northern Portugal into Spanish Galicia to join Marshal Ney's 6th Corps there, both corps could deploy in Estramadura. Marshal Mortier's 5th Corps, currently deployed in central Spain, would also move down. All this was not decided or done at once because of communications and coordination difficulties, but, in the weeks ahead, it all came together.

As it evolved, the French plan to meet the Anglo-Spanish challenge was quite potent. Two corps would be at Talavera to stop the progress of the Anglo-Spanish army. Two to three corps would block the opponent's rear. If the French had some good fortune in spite of their sizeable difficulties in communications, both Wellesley's and Cuesta's armies would be surrounded and, ultimately, destroyed.

French foot artillery gunners, 1808. Print after Vernet and Lami. (Anne S.K. Brown Military Collection, Brown University Library, Providence. Author's photo)

THE BRITISH AND SPANISH

In late June, Marshal Soult wrote to Marshal Ney and King Joseph that he was moving his corps out of Galicia and going south into Leon. His cavalry, now numbering hardly 700 troopers, rode ahead to Zamora led by General of Division Franceschi. Once Zamora was reached, Franceschi decided to ride on ahead to Madrid carrying Soult's dispatches. He trusted his luck and, escorted by only two aides-de-camp, rode out towards Madrid. Luck ran out in the area of Toro where Spanish guerrillas captured him. Soult's dispatches were seized and arrived at the HQ of Wellesley on about 9 July. He now had first-hand information about the positions of the French corps in the north as well as their probable movements. For now, it would be weeks before they could present a substantial threat to the Anglo-Spanish army. This crucial information meant that the campaign could take place. He could thus proceed further east without much fear of being outflanked.

On 10 July, Wellesley and a few of his staff officers rode up some 65km (40 miles), escorted by a squadron of the Spanish Villaviciosa Dragoons to Casa de Miravete near Almaraz to meet Cuesta. Because of a lack of reliable maps, the British general arrived considerably later than planned, sometime after sunset. General Cuesta had planned to start Wellesley's visit with a review of the troops. Thus to greet him, tens of thousands of Spanish soldiers had been under arms for some four hours expecting his arrival at any minute during that long and idle time. The elderly Cuesta had been on his charger at the head of his troops, waiting all that time in spite of still being much annoyed by pains from concussions suffered at the battle of Medellin in March. By the time Wellesley came up, he needed to be supported in the saddle by two pages.

Grenadier corporal, 42nd Highlanders, and grenadier private, 92nd Highlanders. Parts of both of these units contributed men to the 'Battalion of Detachments' that took part in the Talavera campaign. This print after Charles Hamilton Smith was published in July 1812, but the uniforms shown were essentially similar in 1809. (Canadian War Museum, Ottawa. Author's photo)

Brigadier-General Charles Stewart, who accompanied Lt. Gen. Wellesley, later recalled in his *Narrative* that the darkness was lit up by 'an immense number of torches [that] were made to blaze up' all through the Spanish army giving a 'red and wavering light over the whole scene' showing the 'grim and swarthy images of the soldiers, their bright arms and dark uniforms' looking 'peculiarly picturesque as often as the flashes fell upon them'. Although it was now late, Wellesley who had been in the saddle most of the day nevertheless eagerly agreed to review the troops. He was not impressed by what he saw on his first look at a large Spanish army. He immediately perceived a lack of professionalism amongst the officers and a general incapacity for the troops to manoeuvre effectively although there was no doubt that all were in a fighting mood. The troops seen also presented a somewhat ragtag appearance, some being regular troops, but many more being recently organized volunteers, all badly armed and equipped as well as wearing a multitude of uniforms and civilian clothing, and many did not have shoes. Brigadier-General Stewart felt they were 'in the aggregate … little better than bold peasantry, armed partially like soldiers, but completely unacquainted with a soldier's duty.' As for the cavalry, many of the 'horses were good, but the riders manifestly knew nothing of movement or discipline' and had 'miserable equipment, quite unfit for service'. Furthermore, he perceived that, owing to the strict seniority system of promotion of the Spanish, not only Gen. Cuesta, but nearly all the generals with him were 'almost all old men … except for O'Donoju and Zayas' and that they would be 'incapable of bearing the fatigues' of the upcoming campaign. Fortunately, there was a glimmer of hope in that the 'colonels and battalion commanders, appeared to be young and active, and some of whom were … learning to become skilful officers.' But this would be further in the future.

This review seen by torchlight in the evening was further complicated, after all the initial polite contacts and smiles, by the stubborn old general's utter refusal to speak French to Wellesley, the one language they had in common. General Cuesta would not utter one word in French because it was the language of the hated invaders! Fortunately, his army's chief of staff, Gen. O'Donoju, being of Irish ancestry, knew some English and thus now acted as translator. As it were, it was now late and all agreed to go to bed and meet in the morning.

That Wellesley was not especially impressed by what he saw came across in a comment he made to Quartermaster-General Sir George Murray the next day to the effect that he did not know 'what we are to do with these people. Put them behind stone walls' in battle seemed the best option. He now was realizing that his British force was most probably the only regular force in the Peninsula that had a fighting chance against the redoubtable French army.

Leales de Fernando VII Infantry Regiment, 1810. This unit was raised in Talavera from September 1808. It was part of Maj. Gen. R. Manglano's 4th Infantry Division. Watercolour by Antonio Pacheco. (Collection and photo: Biblioteca Publica Municipal, Santa Cruz de Tenerife, Canary Islands)

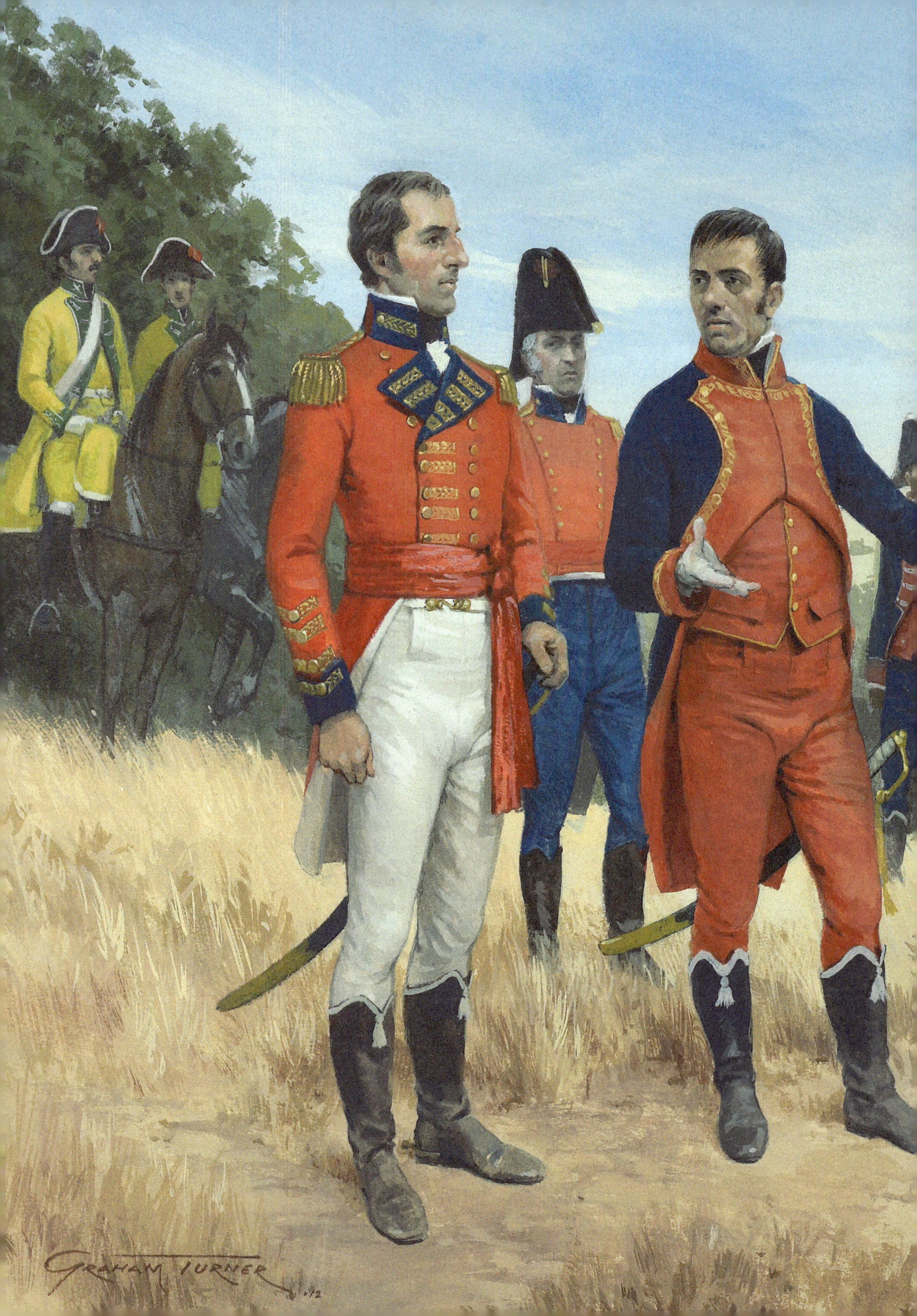
GRAHAM TURNER

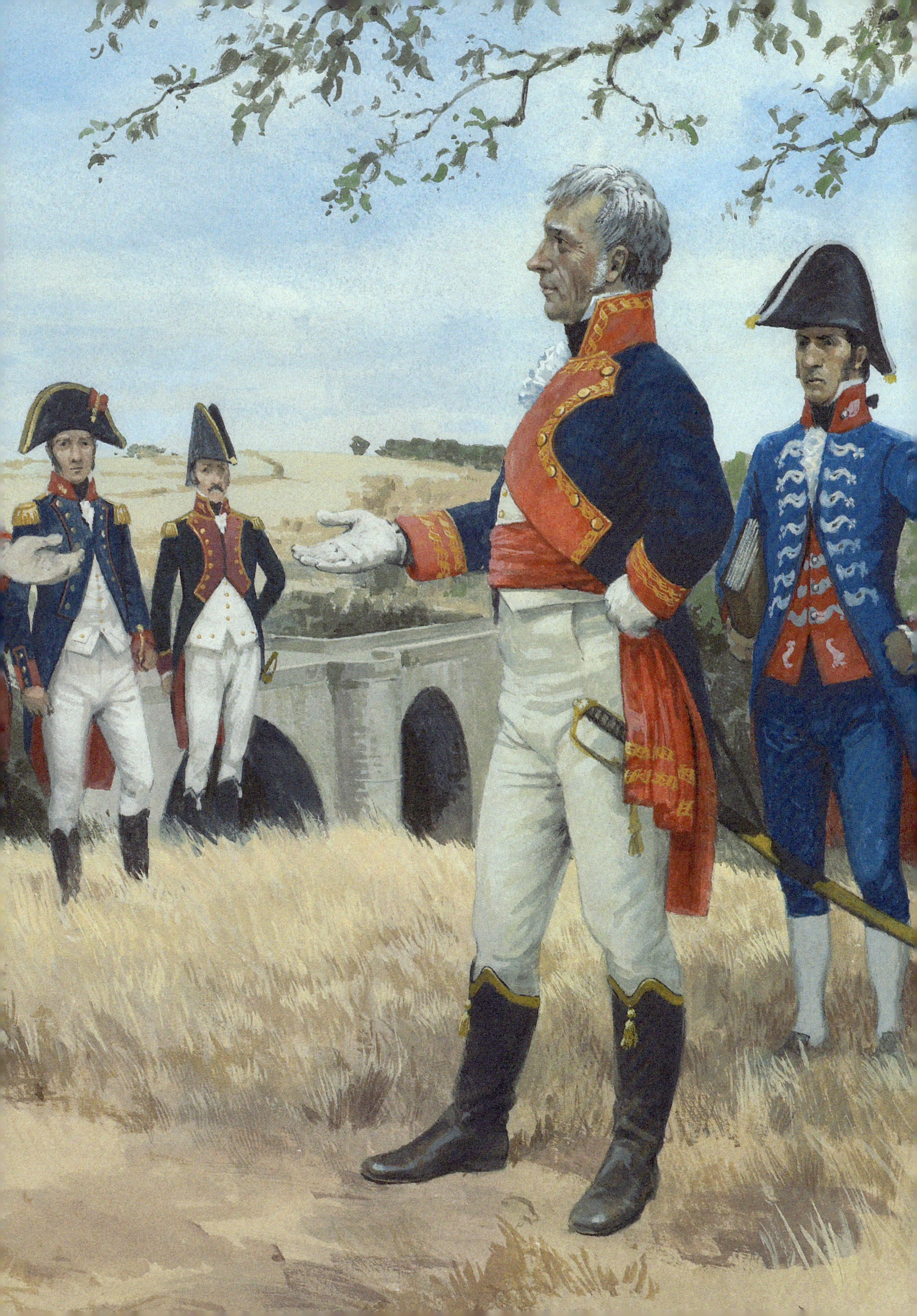

MEETING OF WELLESLEY AND CUESTA, 11 JULY 1809 (PP. 32–33)

This meeting between the allied generals, possibly the most important during the Talavera campaign, turned out to be a very tense affair. It was the first time, for both the British and the Spanish commanders, that senior generals of either nation met to plan the details of a campaign. Neither could speak the other's language and while both knew French, Gen. Cuesta **(1)** would not speak a word of the hated invader's language. Fortunately, the Spanish army's chief of staff, Gen. O'Donoju **(2)**, had Irish origins, knew English and acted as translator. Where the meeting took place on the morning of 11 July is not clear. In the hot Spanish summer, it may well have been on a patio, or better still, near the Tagus River in the shade, to take advantage of a cooling breeze, and it may well have been in the vicinity of Almaraz bridge. The three generals were most likely by themselves with staff officers **(3)** and some escort troops, possibly some of the dragoons **(4)** that had escorted Lt. Gen. Wellesley **(5)** the previous day, looking on in the background. The meeting lasted about four hours, which was unusually long, and turned out to be a frustrating affair for both commanders, although probably more so for Wellesley. He had many strategic and tactical proposals, most of which met with a flat 'No' from Cuesta who was determined not to give any authority to the young British general. But, in spite of frustrations and suspicions, both commanding generals came up with a plan to march east and, hopefully, beat the two opposing French corps separately.

Spanish Light Cavalry trooper, 1809. Print after J. Booth. (Private collection. Author's photo)

The meeting between generals Cuesta and Wellesley got under way on the morning of 11 July. From the start it was a tense affair. Centuries of rivalries between Spain and England could not vanish overnight. The Spanish army observed by Wellesley and his staff officers the previous evening only confirmed the prevailing English opinion regarding vain Spanish pride as well as that nation's ignorance and backwardness. The English were, of course and in their own esteemed opinion, the most modern and forward-looking country in the world, as proved by their country's wealth and genteel lifestyle. To many a Spaniard, this openly expressed attitude by Englishmen merely masked a nation of pirates that had not changed much since the days of Francis Drake.

Whatever the English thought of the Spaniards, Cuesta did not trust these new red-coated allies for a variety of good reasons. Like nearly all Spanish generals, he had, until just over a year before, spent most of his soldier's life mooting operations against the British as enemies; the instant conversion to seeing them as faithful friends was understandably hard to assimilate. The old general had huge suspicions that Sir Arthur would try to make him his second in command and made it clear by his attitude that there was absolutely no question that such an arrangement could ever be entertained. Yet, to many a Briton, this was the only way in the long term to have an effective Spanish force fighting alongside the redcoats.

The bridge at Almaraz that spans the Tagus River. It was near there that Wellesley had his first meeting with Cuesta on 10 and 11 July 1809. (Author's photo)

Another factor deplored by Britons was the near-byzantine state of Spanish politics. In 1809, it was indeed a hotbed of rival factions divided into many semi-independent regional fiefdoms ruled by various local 'juntas' that were supposed to be under the national central assembly, the Central Junta, that was currently sitting in Sevilla trying to provide a national government in the name of Fernando VII, the would-be king who had been kidnapped by Napoleon. The Central Junta had few real powers outside of Sevilla's city limits; real power was largely wielded by the various generals whose only restraint was that their appointments as commanders had to be blessed by the central assembly; hence the existence of various generals' factions vying for power and influence from Central Junta members. There was thus great rivalry between the various leading generals.

As Gen. O'Donoju got under way, translating Sir Arthur's proposals, Gen. Cuesta silently felt he could not cede an inch to his young, new ally. That he did not trust Wellesley is obvious, but he trusted possibly even less some of his own fellow Spanish generals. The main 1809 contenders were, besides Cuesta, the Duke of Infantendo, the Duke of Albuquerque and Gen. Venegas, these last two being practically 'at daggers drawn' with the old general now facing Sir Arthur. Insofar as he was concerned, he had supreme command; he was in his own country and had the larger army. Thus, he was deeply suspicious of the proposals now made by Sir Arthur.

The general plan was to unite both armies and march on Madrid by following the upper Tagus River Valley to Toledo, then head up to the Spanish capital. To this, Gen. Cuesta could only agree. He also concurred that a reinforcement from his army would be sent north to help hold the passes at Perales and Baños. At this time, a French move from the north was not expected by the Anglo-Spanish command according to the intelligence available.

What was then unknown was the reaction of the French to the British army's entry into Spanish Estramadura. In fact, the strategy to meet the challenge was already being implemented. Marshal Mortier's 5th Corps was moving west, past Salamanca, and would turn south towards Estramadura. Marshal Soult's 2nd Corps and Ney's 6th Corps were also marching south from Galicia.

But, on 11 July, none of this had materialized. Sir Arthur's first proposal concerned sending 10,000 of Gen. Cuesta's men north to look for Marshal Mortier, a move that would also threaten the French in Madrid itself. General Cuesta's answer was a flat 'No' – there was no question of weakening his army. Instead, Lt. Gen. Wellesley could detach 10,000 men from his army if he wished. This represented half of the British force and was of course unrealistic. A compromise of sorts was finally reached by detaching Sir Robert Wilson's 1,500 Portuguese with 2,000 Spaniards to act as a forward force north-east of the allied main army.

Troopers of the Spanish Villaviciosa and Pavia dragoon regiments, c.1805–1809. A detachment of the Villaviciosa Dragoons provided Wellesley's escort when he travelled to meet Cuesta at Almaraz on 10 and 11 July 1809. It is shown in the 1805 dress regulation uniform that was still worn by many older Spanish units in 1809. Print after R. Knotel. (Private collection. Author's photo)

Sir Robert Wilson, commanding the Portuguese and Spanish detachment operating further north and east following the 11 July meeting between generals Wellesley and Cuesta. (Private collection. Author's photo)

Another important strategic aim was to involve Gen. Venegas and his army of La Mancha, which numbered some 26,000 men. If he moved on Gen. Sébastiani's 4th Corps of 15,000 men in the vicinity of Toledo while Wellesley's and Cuesta's 56,000 men marched east, a potential force of 82,000 troops would close around an estimated 35,000 French troops led by Marshal Victor and King Joseph. Should Sébastiani decide to rally Victor instead of fighting Venegas, then Venegas's army was to liberate Madrid, then join Wellesley's and Cuesta's armies to attack both French corps. The odds would be about two against one in favour of the Anglo-Spanish. Although there were issues between Sir Arthur and Gen. Cuesta on some details, both felt this was a decent strategic plan; if it worked, it could result in the defeat and perhaps even the destruction of two French army corps involving some 50,000 men. That would have been a major setback for Napoleon who was then leading most of his army in a difficult campaign against Austria and thus hardly in a position to send reinforcements to Spain. So, in spite of all the suspicions about each other, Sir Arthur and Gen. Cuesta had come up with a remarkably good course of action. There was, however, an unknown factor in the plan: what the commander of the army of La Mancha, Gen. Venegas, who was Gen. Cuesta's bitter political rival, would think of this strategy.

THE TALAVERA CAMPAIGN

THE AREA OF THE COMING BATTLE

From mid-July, the three armies were moving in various spots along the upper Tagus River valley between Oropesa for the British and Spanish, and Toledo and Madrid for the French. The focal point of all this military activity was the city of Talavera de la Reyna, situated right in the middle of the area. As the armies gathered and approached each other, it became increasingly obvious that the city or its immediate area would become the scene of the clash. The questions that remained were exactly where and when.

General of Division Franceschi, cavalry commander of Marshal Soult's 2nd French Army Corps. He was captured in early July 1809 by El Capucino's Spanish Guerrillas on his way to Madrid carrying Marshal Soult's dispatches. These were rushed to Lt. Gen. Wellesley and provided him with invaluable information about the pursuit of the Talavera campaign. Contemporary print. (Anne S.K. Brown Military Collection, Brown University Library, Providence. Author's photo)

Armies converge on Talavera, July 1809

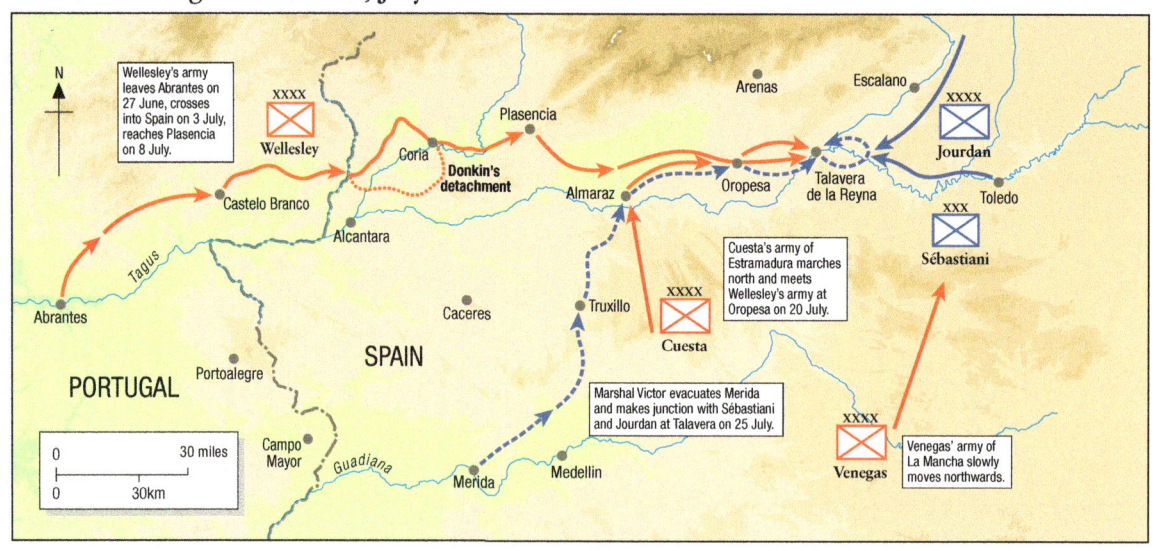

Talavera de la Reyna is situated at the southern end of the province (or 'kingdom') of Old Castilla. The city was in a sorry state during the summer of 1809. It had been a thriving centre of ceramics manufacture with a population of about 10,000 souls, but the successive passages of the French armies, who were prone to looting and rape, had driven part of its population to seek refuge in the northern hills. Many houses were now abandoned and had been broken into by marauding soldiers who, quite apart from whatever they might pocket, found that furniture left therein made excellent firewood. The churches had also suffered from the rather unholy visitors of the French army; the cathedral, after having been liberated of whatever gold or silver objects it contained, had been left somewhat alone and the fine Murillo painting enhancing its altar had not overly tempted the connoisseurs of the French army; another church, however, had been totally devastated by its conversion into a French infantry barracks. On the whole, this once-prosperous city was now a mere shadow of its former self.

Edging the city to the south was the Tagus River, which was spanned by a long bridge and a road leading to the shrine town of Guadalupe in the mountains further south. The roads to Madrid and Toledo to the west and to Estramadura and Andalusia further east and south ran along the valley on the northern bank of the Tagus. That was where the armies marched and it was where the forthcoming battle would be fought, just outside Talavera. The city's surrounding terrain on the northern side of the Tagus River was lush and cultivated at that time, consisting mainly of olive groves and some plantations of cork trees. This plain area ran north for some 2–2.5km, until the rising ground of the Cerra de Medellin and the Cerra de Cascajal was encountered. Over these hills came another, much smaller, Northern Plain that was bordered on its northern side by the higher Sierra de Segurilla mountain range. Various streams from that Sierra flowed onto the Northern Plain and formed into the narrow Portala River, which then flowed south and went through the city of Talavera to meet the Tagus River.

The road west of Talavera led to Oropesa, some 35km away, and on to Almaraz and Estramadura. Four and a half kilometres east of Talavera, the road arrived at the banks of the Albreche River that was spanned by a bridge. On the other side were two roads, one leading to Madrid some 130km away, the other to Toledo at about 65km due east.

With the armies getting closer to each other as they marched eastwards, their scouts would run into each other. On 21 July, the Spanish forward corps ran into a sizeable French force near Gamonal, west of Talavera, and the inconclusive shooting lasted for about four hours until the French retreated when British cavalry arrived on the scene. The Spanish were not very keen on putting up a determined fight, which exasperated Brig. Gen. Stewart who wanted to press the French rearguard. Most of Marshal Victor's army had already crossed the Albreche River east of Talavera. In the afternoon, Lt. Gen. Wellesley reached the bank of the river. Marshal Victor, while retreating further east, warned Madrid that the British army was right behind the Spanish. Up to 22 July, King Joseph and Marshal Jourdan did not know that Wellesley's British army had entered Spain. Orders were sent at once for Gen. Sébastiani's 4th Corps to join Marshal Victor.

Wellesley wanted to attack as soon as possible while Marshal Victor's corps was still by itself and planned to do so on 23 July, but Gen. Cuesta did not agree and the operation was cancelled, much to the disappointment of the British. The Spanish general changed his mind the next day and his troops advanced further east to attack Victor's troops; the British were further behind, east of Talavera. On 25 July, however, Gen. Cuesta learned that 4th Corps and also King Joseph's guard reserve had now joined Marshal Victor's army. The opportunity to beat each French corps separately had vanished. Realizing that only the Spanish army faced them, marshals Victor and Jourdan ordered their troops to march west and engage the Spaniards. General Cuesta beat a hasty retreat and got back to the banks of the Albreche River after losing about 400 men. The next day, the British advanced to the river to cover the Spanish retreat. The Anglo-Spanish army was to be deployed between Talavera and the northern hills, this position having been chosen by Lt. Gen. Wellesley.

The fields west of Talavera. The British and Spanish forces marched through and met the French in this general area on 27 July 1809. This was probably the general appearance of the battlefield, which is now mostly transformed and built over. (Author's photo)

THE BATTLE OF TALAVERA, 27 JULY

The Anglo-Spanish army considered making a stand west of the Albreche River. The Spanish army finished crossing the Albreche River during the morning using both the bridge and the river, which was then rather low being in the middle of a hot Spanish summer. Keeping the summer heat in mind, the French had broken up their camp at about two in the morning in order to march more comfortably in the cooler night air. Their field guns occasionally fired on the Spanish, but with little effect owing to the distance. At noon, the French appeared formed in columns, the men already suffering from the sun's effects. They now came in sight of Anson's cavalry and of Sherbrooke's and Mackenzie's British infantry divisions who shot a few distant volleys at them before they withdrew from Cazalegas in echelon, crossed the Albreche River, and lined up on its eastern bank in the general area of an old building called Casa de Salinas. From a distance, the French thought it was yet another Spanish convent with its little bell-like towers, but it was actually a farming estate.

Wellesley was on the spot in one of the estate's towers looking over the area. He had chosen a position further west to deploy his army between the Tagus River and a pointed hill to the north called the Cerro de Medellin. However, the area between the Albreche River and this new position was covered with cork and olive groves, the trees of which nearly totally hid whatever was further east, and that was the French army! The allied army moved further west to the new positions on the far banks of the narrow Portina River, except for Mackenzie's division that acted as a rearguard in the area of the Casa de Salinas.

Carabinier and chasseur of 9th French Light Infantry Regiment, c.1807. This unit was part of Gen. Ruffin's 1st Division in Marshal Victor's 1st Corps. Otto manuscript. (Anne S.K. Brown Military Collection, Brown University Library, Providence. Author's photo)

The British scouts thought that there was little danger and that only French cavalrymen were in the woods. In fact, Marshal Victor's infantrymen had already reached the Albreche River and men from Gen. Lapisse's division were crossing the river north of Casa de Salinas where Wellesley was located, but he had not seen the French troops. Suddenly, musketry fire broke out nearby as the French soldiers ran into the British troops. Not wasting an instant, Wellesley rushed down the tower's stairway, jumped on his horse and galloped away, barely escaping the French *voltigeurs*. One may wonder what the course of the Napoleonic Wars might have been should they have captured or slain him.

In the event he got away safely, but some of the surprised British troops were not as lucky. In the confused withdrawal of four regiments, the British lost some 442 men including nearly a hundred soldiers made prisoner by the French. Other troops came to the rescue and Mackenzie's division made an orderly retreat to take up its new position west of the Portina River.

Meanwhile, the British and the Spanish were forming their lines of defence along both shores of the narrow Portina River from the city going north right up to the Cerro de Medellin. The Spanish army was posted east of the city and to its north on both sides of the Portina River up to about half of the southern plain at Pajar de Vergara where the British positions started and where, on the east bank of the river, an artillery battery had been built flanked by Campbell's brigade to its north. The successive British infantry and cavalry brigades ran past the Cerro de Medellin to the edge of the Northern Plain.

With Marshal Victor's 1st Corps leading, the French army crossed the Albreche River and moved west towards the positions of the Anglo-Spanish army. The 1st Corps was ahead and swiftly occupied the upper half of the southern plain, Gen. Ruffin's division securing the Cerro de Cascajal. His gunners and sappers started the construction of a large battery on its flat top. The Cerro de Cascajal was about 45m high. It was about 30m lower than the height of the Cerro de Medellin, past the western bank of the Portina River. Lieutenant-General Sherbrooke's division was to occupy the northern end and assigned the Guards brigade to the defence of the left flank of the allied army. However, the centre was without defenders because Maj. Gen. Mackenzie's division was late in arriving, having covered the retreat from Casa de Salinas. So, during the early evening, Sherbrooke's division including the Guards secured the centre and Mackenzie's division moved to the northern end instead. Further east was Hill's division in the second line.

Facing Mackenzie's division was Gen. Ruffin's which could not see that Col. Donkin's British brigade from Mackenzie's division was on the other side of the hill. What redcoats he did see were the Löw's and Langwerth's King's German Legion brigades which were just arriving exhausted from much marching and, as darkness fell, thought that they were in the second line and promptly laid down in their blankets to get some sleep, but they were actually posted in the first line facing the French. Thus there was confusion about which unit was where and Lt. Gen. Wellesley had some trouble figuring out the positions actually taken by his troops but, on the whole, the British presented a front that would be difficult to attack. The Spanish troops were also well disposed in three lines, the first east of the Portina River going from the battery at Pajar de Vergara to the town of Talavera de la Reyna with two more lines west of the river. Another contingent was west of the city behind an artillery battery.

At about seven in the evening, some French dragoons appeared at the distant edges of the olive groves in front of Gen. Portago's Spanish infantry situated at about the lower middle of the allied army's line. As was their custom, the French dragoons galloped a bit closer, fired their pistols, and galloped back into the groves for cover. This somewhat 'standard procedure' produced amazement and shock in many of the men in the Spanish battalions, who were obviously quite 'green' and insufficiently trained for what must have been their first engagement.

Grenadier and fusilier of 96th French Line Infantry Regiment, c.1807. This unit was part of Gen. Ruffin's 1st Division in Marshal Victor's 1st Corps. Otto manuscript. (Anne S.K. Brown Military Collection, Brown University Library, Providence. Author's photo)

They now levelled their muskets and fired a tremendous volley all along their line into the now-deserted olive groves. Many men could not see what was happening and, unsteadied by their own musketry's sounds and all the smoke, panicked and, shouting treason, four battalions broke up and turned, dropping their muskets to run faster!

In the general free-for-all, many pillaged British supply convoys in their path and the panic even spread to Gen. Cuesta's own carriage drivers. Lieutenant-General Wellesley, wondering what was going on south of his army, galloped to the Spanish HQ to find out and, seeing it was a false alarm, asked that the firing be stopped. Ashamed and very angry Gen. Cuesta succeeded in holding the firing back, then sent his cavalry to rally the fleeing soldiers although several hundreds managed to get away. Of those brought back, many had been forced to turn back by the points of the cavalrymen's swords. An outraged Cuesta decreed that a hundred men, with their officers, would be executed by firing squads after the upcoming battle. Wellesley intervened that he should relent, but Cuesta was truly enraged and merely agreed not to execute as many. Three days later, six officers and 34 soldiers were duly executed.

Certainly the most positive aspect of this incident was that the French had not realized what was going on in front of them in the Spanish sector. Even if they had, the positions of most of the French army could hardly have exploited the sudden gap in the Spanish line, which was soon filled by battalions of Gen. Cuesta's second line. The French were still too far away to mount an attack there although their artillery's long-range rounds could reach some of the Anglo-Spanish front lines. By mid-evening of the 27th, Gen. Ruffin's brigade and the light artillery of Victor's 1st Corps were moving into place at the northern flank of the French line with the rest of the division about to take its positions further south, but Gen. Sébastiani's 4th Corps was still about 2km east of the Portola River as it marched west. King Joseph's reserve from Madrid was further back at Casa de Salinas. The French artillery then stopped shooting. It seemed that the day's actions were done as darkness fell and that the real battle would be saved for the next day.

Victor attacks

However, Marshal Victor saw it otherwise. He was one of those redoubtable commanders that would moot a daring attack when his opponent did not expect it; with luck, such actions could destabilize an enemy army and that was exactly what he now was preparing. From the Cerro de Cascajal that was about 45m high, he looked at the dispositions of the British troops in front of him on and to the south of the Cerro de Medellin hill past the western bank of the Portina River. He could see Löw's and Langwerth's brigades and some of Donkin's. To his amazement, the top of the Cerro de Medellin in front of him was not yet occupied by British or Spanish troops. He immediately saw an opportunity to attack the British northern flank. What he did not appear to have fully realized was that the Cerro de Medellin was about 30m higher than where he was standing so that he could not see parts of Hill's division that were further away on the other side. All the same, his calculation was good from what he could see. The opponent seen consisted of the four King's German Legion battalions that had laid down to sleep, and the 87th and 88th Foot totalling two battalions that had already been mauled earlier at Casa de Salinas and who were equally tired. Thus, there were only six British battalions visible in the immediate area and none of them on top of the strategically located Cerro de Medellin. But night was falling fast.

Ruffin's nine battalions were certainly also tired having been up and marching since two in the morning, but they were in excellent spirits and formed up in the darkness. The 9th Light Infantry was at the centre flanked by the 24th Line Infantry to the north and 96th Line infantry to its south. Marshal Victor's plan was simply to have the 9th charge right through the 87th and 88th Foot and gain the summit of the Cerro de Medellin. This attack would be supported by the two French line infantry regiments that would sweep whatever was in the way and secure the hill. Now outflanked with that hill captured, this night attack might force the Anglo-Spanish army to withdraw and seek a new position, hopefully in much confusion. Victor wished to act immediately to secure the Cerro de Medellin before the British could do so and did not ask King Joseph's and Marshal Jourdan's opinions; they might not have agreed and, in any event, the opportunity would likely have vanished by the time he would have received an answer.

When the French moved on, it was about ten in the evening and night had fallen. In the darkness, the 9th Light Infantry veered somewhat to the south and ran into sleeping, or half asleep, infantrymen in the forward posts of Löw's brigade who sounded the alarm even as they were swept over the French light infantrymen; those that managed to retreat were further mauled by a volley from the alarmed 7th King's German Legion's battalion that, in the darkness, mistook its comrades running towards them for the enemy. Confusion now overtook both the 5th and 7th King's German Legion battalions as the crowd of men running towards them were indeed French soldiers making a bayonet attack; the shock was severe and, in a few minutes, the surprised German battalions started to give way after losing some 109 killed and wounded and 88 captured. The 96th French Line Regiment should have now arrived to complete the piercing of the British line, which would have created a critical situation for Wellesley, but it had been delayed in its movement at the crossing and then stopped when spotted and fired upon by some troops of Langwerth's brigade. The 96th was thus disoriented in the dark. Meanwhile, the 24th French Line Regiment got lost in the darkness north of the Cerro de Medellin and never encountered any British troops, being too far from its objective and ignorant of where it really was.

Major-General Rowland Hill. He commanded the 2nd British Division and, on the night of 27 July, led the counter-attack against Marshal Victor's surprise assault. Hill was one of Gen. Wellesley's finest and most trusted officers who served in all campaigns in the Peninsula and at Waterloo. From 1828 to 1839, he succeeded the Duke of Wellington as commander-in-chief of the Forces. Print from the 1830s. (Private collection. Author's photo)

Note: Gridlines are shown at intervals of 1km

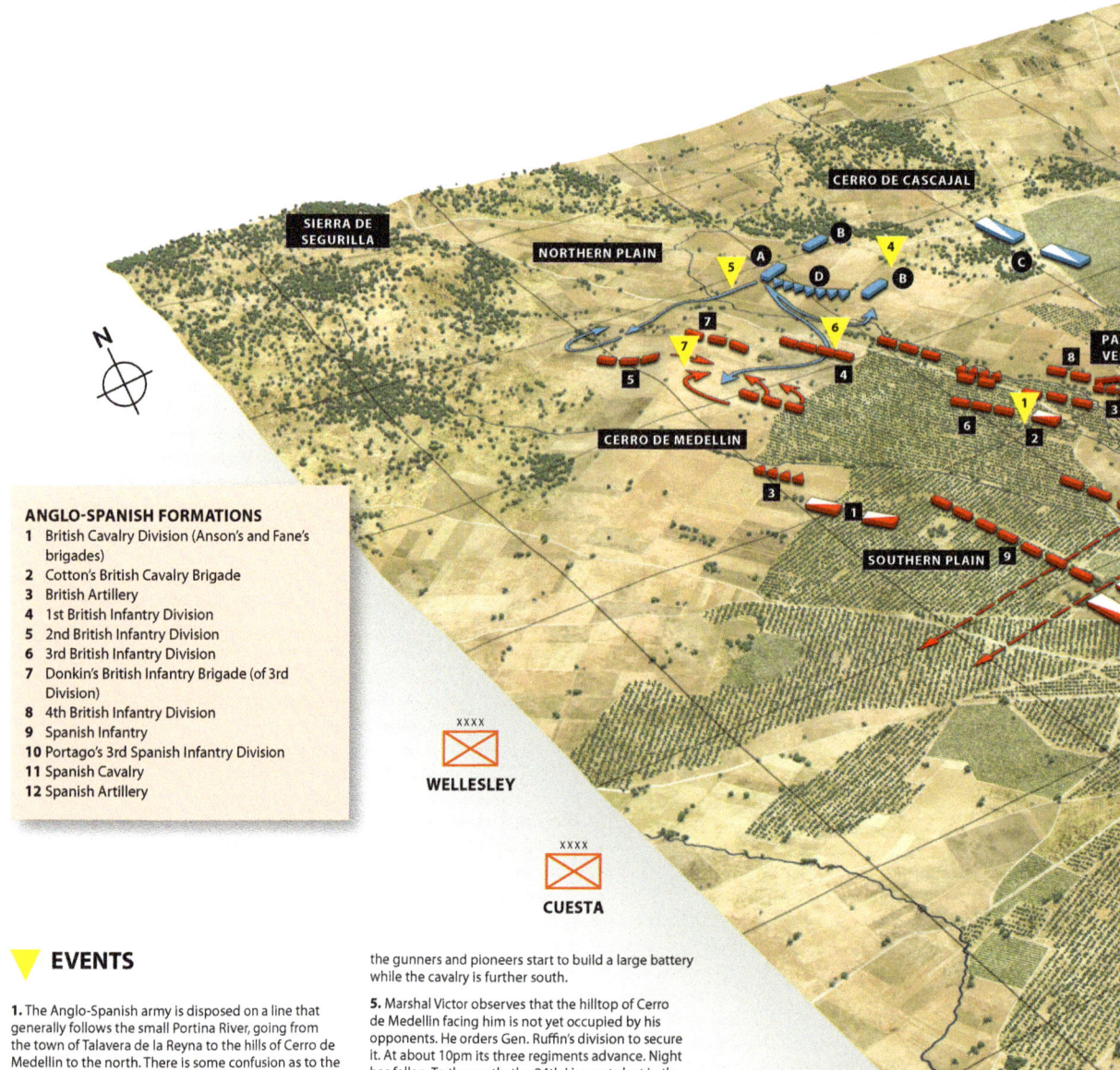

ANGLO-SPANISH FORMATIONS
1. British Cavalry Division (Anson's and Fane's brigades)
2. Cotton's British Cavalry Brigade
3. British Artillery
4. 1st British Infantry Division
5. 2nd British Infantry Division
6. 3rd British Infantry Division
7. Donkin's British Infantry Brigade (of 3rd Division)
8. 4th British Infantry Division
9. Spanish Infantry
10. Portago's 3rd Spanish Infantry Division
11. Spanish Cavalry
12. Spanish Artillery

▼ EVENTS

1. The Anglo-Spanish army is disposed on a line that generally follows the small Portina River, going from the town of Talavera de la Reyna to the hills of Cerro de Medellin to the north. There is some confusion as to the exact disposition of the Guards and the King's German Legion while the highest hill is not secured. By about mid-evening, the British forces occupy the northern half of the Anglo-Spanish army's position. The Spanish army occupies the southern half, about a third of it on the east side of the Portola River.

2. At about 7pm, a French vanguard party of mounted dragoons emerges from the trees in front of General Portago's Spanish infantry. The dragoons gallop a bit closer, fires their pistols at the startled Spaniards, and safely gallop back into the groves for cover. This creates havoc and a general panic in some four Spanish battalions whose 2,000 men break and run wildly back while other troops fired volleys at the woods, but the French dragoons are already vanished.

3. Lt. Gen. Wellesley hears the firing in the Spanish sector, rides down to Gen. Cuesta and both stop the firing and re-form the Spanish line.

4. Marshal Victor and his French 1st Corps are the first to arrive close to the Anglo-Spanish position. The three infantry divisions secure the Cerro de Cascajal where the gunners and pioneers start to build a large battery while the cavalry is further south.

5. Marshal Victor observes that the hilltop of Cerro de Medellin facing him is not yet occupied by his opponents. He orders Gen. Ruffin's division to secure it. At about 10pm its three regiments advance. Night has fallen. To the north, the 24th Line gets lost in the darkness well above its target and eventually turns back. To the south, the 96th Line also gets disoriented and bogged down in the Portina River banks, and finally turns back. At the centre, the 9th Light Infantry, however, is on target.

6. The 9th Light Infantry quickly overcomes the King's German Legion's forward guards and then burst upon its 5th and 7th Battalions, whose exhausted men are already asleep, overruns them and starts up the Cerro de Medellin.

7. Maj. Gen. Hill brings up Stewart's brigade and leads it against the oncoming French at the head of the 29th Foot, secures the top of the Cerro de Medellin and attacks the French. Tilson's brigade is also coming up. The French put up a fierce fight, but are outnumbered and retreat back to the Cerro de Cascajal. Marshal Victor's attack failed, but it was a hard fought close call; had the 24th and 96th Line not gotten lost in the dark, it is likely that the Anglo-Spanish army would have been attacked on its northern flank. Wellesley was very lucky that evening.

FRENCH FORMATIONS
- **A** Ruffin's 1st French Infantry Division (1st Army Corps)
- **B** 2nd and 3rd French Infantry Divisions (1st Army Corps)
- **C** Cavalry of French 1st Army Corps
- **D** French Artillery
- **E** French Dragoon Vanguard
- **F** French 4th Army Corps

TALAVERA, EVENING OF 27 JULY 1809

The Anglo-Spanish army marching east under the command of generals Wellesley and Cuesta is met at Talavera by a French army under the nominal command of King Joseph, but actually led by marshals Jourdan and Victor. They get there during the late afternoon and evening of 27 July. The Anglo-Spanish army takes up position along the Portina River from the Tagus River northwards to the Cerro de Medellin. The first element of the French army to face the allied army is Marshal Victor's 1st Army Corps. After an initial panic by some Spanish troops, Victor notes a flaw in Wellesley's dispositions at the Cerro de Medellin.

Upon hearing the shooting, Wellesley, who seemingly was then near the Spanish troops to the south, then hurried up to the scene of the action. His division commanders had already taken measures to secure the position. Lieutenant-General Sherbrooke was keeping Cameron's brigade ready to intervene while Maj. Gen. Hill moved his division east to climb the Cerro de Medellin. What happened next, as seen from the French side, is related by one of their soldiers, Girod de l'Ain of 9th Light Infantry: 'We had already climbed two thirds of the height without encountering any enemies when we suddenly received a terrible musketry volley that made many casualties among us in a few instants.' The brave Frenchmen rallied to the cry of '*Vive l'Empereur*' and continued their ascent, but when they neared the top, they were met by more British troops emerging in the darkness. The counter-attack had been swiftly organized by Maj. Gen. Hill by sending the 48th Foot's 1st Battalion to Löw's rescue. He somewhat believed that it might be a false alarm, but he soon perceived that this was indeed a real French attack. When he arrived on the spot, his horse was struck by a bullet and a French soldier even got hold of his horse's bridle, but 'the general,' wrote Napier, 'spurring the animal hard, broke the man's hold' and galloped down to safety meeting the 29th Foot that was coming up into action.

General of Division François Amable Ruffin, *c.*1809–1811. He commanded the 1st Division of Marshal Victor's 1st Corps. Watercolour by Pierre Albert Leroux. (Anne S.K. Brown Military Collection, Brown University Library, Providence. Author's photo)

Hill now mustered the three battalions of Stewart's brigade in his division and put himself at the head of the 29th Foot. The 48th and 1st Battalions of Detachments, which were mostly composed of Highlanders, also moved on the French in the darkness; the men on both sides could guess friend or foe only from the gleam of musket flashes in the night. The French battalions of the 9th Light Infantry knew an enemy force was moving up; some of its men shouted they were Spaniards, others said they were Germans, but the three battalions were actually British and managed to advance in line. The British skirmishers were ahead and, in the dark, would shout 'English?' to unknown shadows, according to Girod de l'Ain, to which the French would answer '*Anglais! Anglais!*' according to Lt. Close of the 48th Foot. The British soon fired volleys in the dark and a struggle in the night with the French 9th Light Infantry ensued. Girod de l'Ain of the 9th further noted that 'about 200 Scots wearing skirts were captured' which seems a high number. They were obviously from the 1st Battalion of Detachments, but they were soon released when the order to withdraw was given by the French commander who realized the game was up and that he was outnumbered. Girod de l'Ain recalled, 'we went down the cliff of the hill, somewhat in disorder'. Meanwhile, the 29th Foot reached the summit and planted its colours on the highest point. Major-General Hill now had the Cerro de Medellin secured and did not pursue. The French 9th Light Infantry actually stopped and re-formed at about midway down the hill and sent men back up to carry down their wounded men that could be found, the others further up being taken prisoner by the British.

The 9th Light Infantry had been heavily engaged and lost some 300 men, including 65 made prisoner, and amongst them was its wounded commander, Col. Meunier. The British casualties were also at about 300 men of which a third were of the King's German Legion made prisoners, most likely when, early in the attack, the French 9th Light Infantry burst onto the sleeping German infantrymen. Major-General Hill had also been wounded by a bullet that grazed his head causing a commotion. He passed on his command to Brig. Gen. Tilson and retired from the field.

Marshal Victor's attack had failed on account of the darkness and unfamiliarity with the terrain, as far as it could be seen. Because of this, two out of the three attacking regiments had not participated in the action, being bogged down and lost in the dark. However, the three battalions of the 9th Light Infantry that did reach their objective sent shivers down the spines of the British commanders. The 9th rolled over two German battalions, generally considered good troops, and it had taken another three British battalions to push the French back. The other problem for Marshal Victor's attack was that it had not been sufficiently supported by other French troops. On the other hand, the British had been very lucky that only one in three French infantrymen had actually been able to make the attack. One cannot be too optimistic about what would have happened to the British positions if all nine French battalions had been fully engaged. Furthermore, the British troops behaved somewhat carelessly regarding their forward outposts so that when the French attacked it was too late and they were upon the encamped men in a few instants. The inaction of Donkin's brigade, which seems to have kept its position instead of giving a helping hand to Hill's battalions, would indicate some confusion on the part of its division commander, Maj. Gen. Mackenzie.

The Cerro de Medellin hill where Wellesley deployed some of his troops that were unseen by the French and their artillery. It is situated north of the motorway and is now a private estate with a swimming pool occupying the ground where the British troops were situated. Nearby, the modest-sized obelisk put on the site in 1909 to commemorate the battle's centennial, is visible as a small dart against the sky in the centre. (Author's photo)

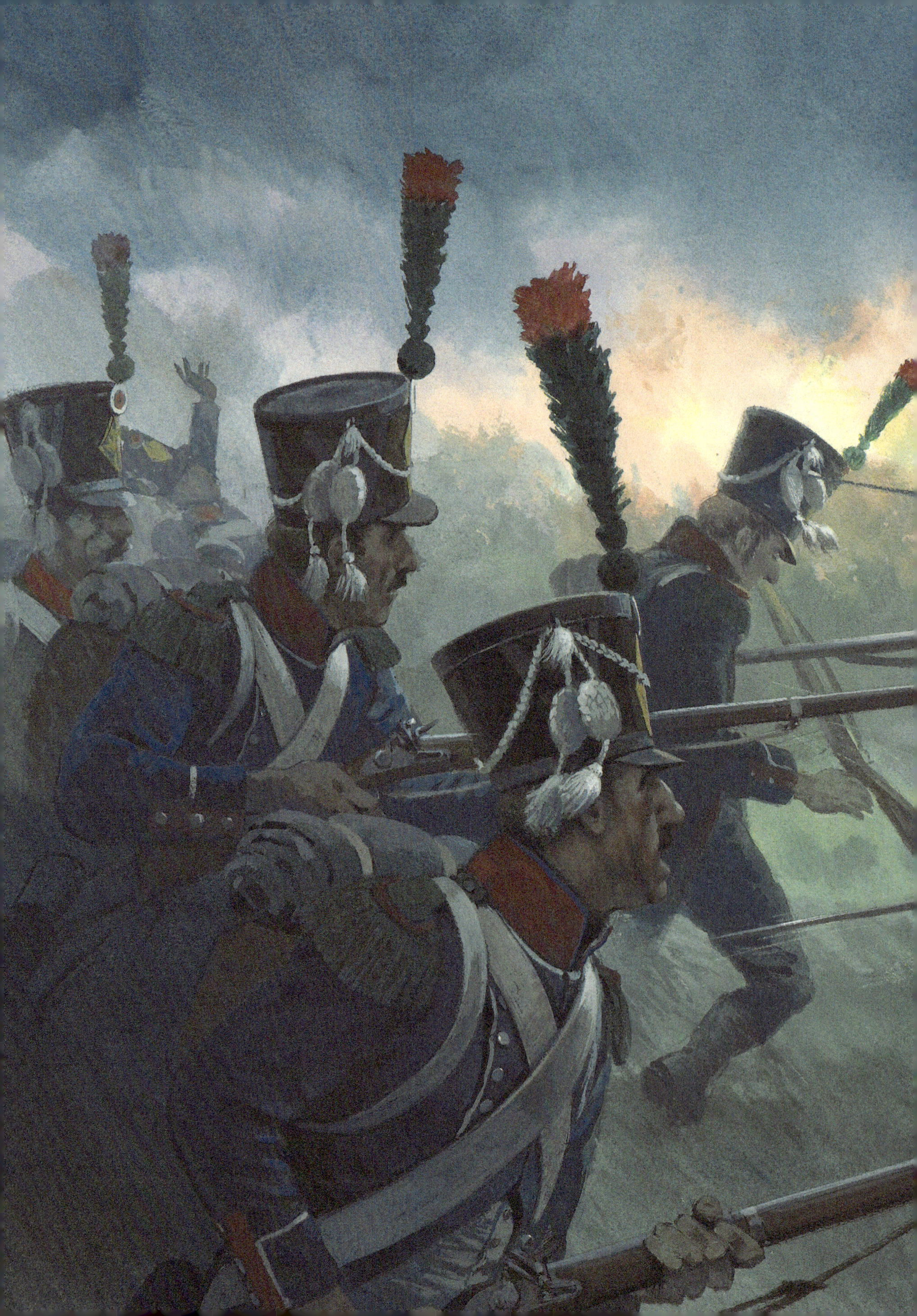

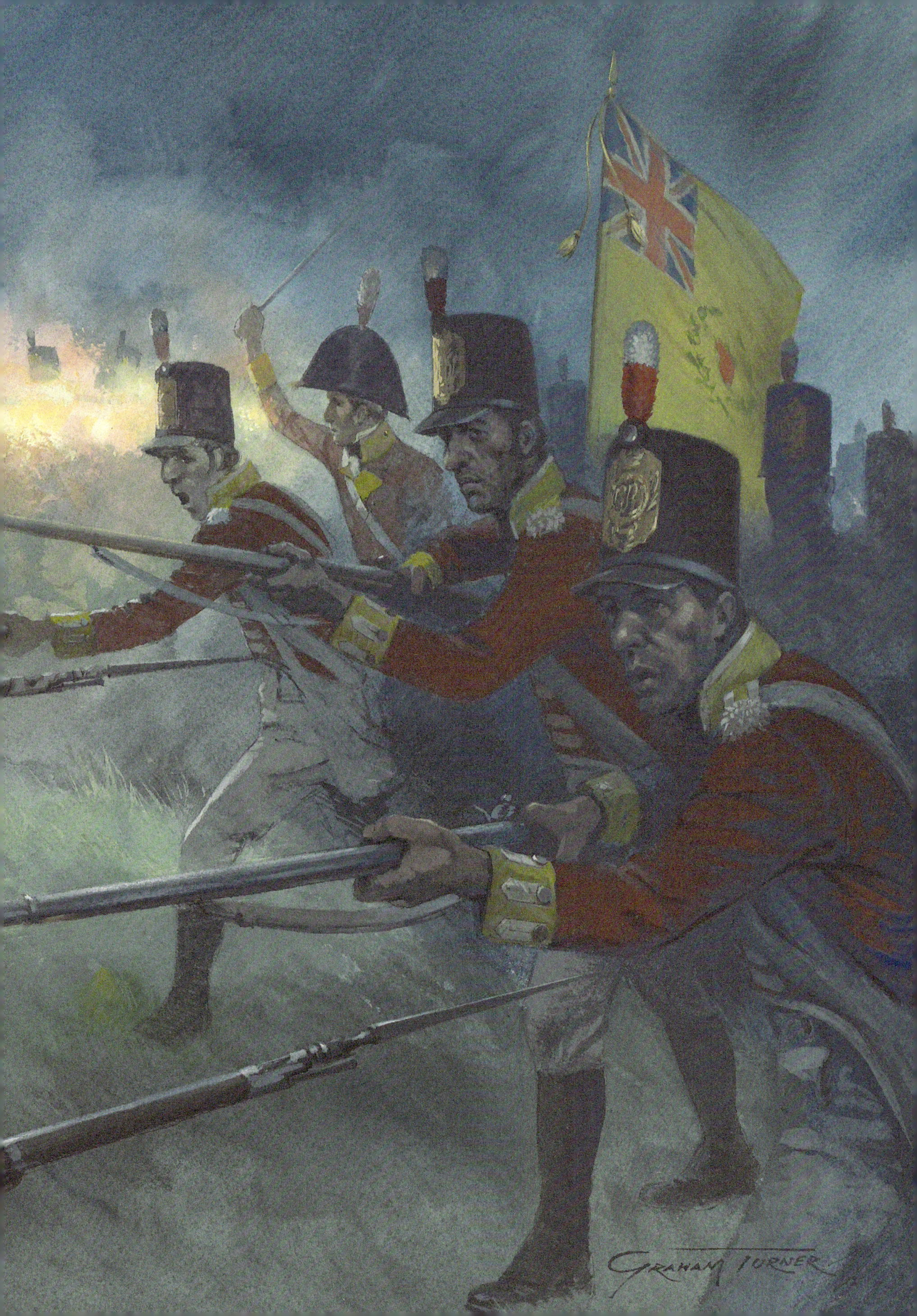
GRAHAM TURNER

THE BRITISH SECURE THE CERRO DE MEDELLIN (PP. 50–51)

On the evening of 27 July, Marshall Victor, whose 1st Corps first arrived opposite the Anglo-Spanish army, resolved to attack the British at once, having perceived the weakness of the northern flank of the allied army's position; the Cerro de Medellin – the highest hill to the north – had not yet been secured. It was very fortunate for Gen. Wellesley that two out of three of the attacking regiments lost their way in the dark and were not engaged. The one that did was 9th Light Infantry **(1)** whose three battalions turned out to be quite a match. They overran two battalions of the King's German Legion and ascended towards the top of the Cerro de Medellin. Fortunately for the British, generals Sherbrooke and Hill reacted efficiently to bring up troops to oppose the French. There now occurred a desperate battle in the dark lit only by musket flashes. At last, the 29th Foot **(2)** reached the summit and planted its colours on the highest point. The French finally retreated. The British had secured the Cerro de Medellin after a very hard fight and did not pursue. It may have been the most important engagement of the battle of Talavera. Had the British lost it, it is likely the Anglo-Spanish army would have had to withdraw.

Finally, Lt. Gen. Wellesley, the commander-in-chief, was not on the spot at any time during this night action, being further south and probably with the Spanish staff. On hearing the gunfire, Wellesley did go up and arrived after the French had been repulsed by Sherbrooke's and Hill's troop movements. Events of the attack suggest that, in any case, Wellesley was unlikely to have been able to do anything spectacular in the dark. As it were, his lieutenants had reacted successfully to the threat with the help, it must be stressed, of a great deal of good luck in that two-thirds of the French attacking force got lost in the night. Marshal Victor had nevertheless seen the gap in the British position and Wellesley immediately posted three brigades (Stewart's, Tilson's and Donkin's) on the Cerro de Medellin and proper outposts all along the line. He learned his lessons from Victor quickly and applied them for the rest of his military campaigns.

Sometime after midnight, Marshal Victor's first ADC, Col. Huguet-Châteaux, galloped over to King Joseph's HQ at Casa de Salinas to tell him that 1st Corps' attack had failed, but that Victor would renew the attack the next day. King Joseph listened to the ADC's report and thanked him, but had no answers or instructions for 1st Corps. He basically felt, like his military mentor Marshal Jourdan, that it was best not to engage the enemy now. Marshal Soult was known to be marching south and would thus arrive to the rear of the Anglo-Spanish army, but the question was when. The corps of marshals Mortier and Ney were also marching down to join Soult so that the French would enjoy overwhelming superiority in the area. One big worry on King Joseph's mind was the safety of Madrid itself, in which he had left a skeleton garrison while Toledo was also very weakly manned with only Gen. Valence's weakened division. Should there be uprisings in these cities, combined with an advance from Gen. Vanegas's Spanish troops further south, Madrid itself might be lost and this was unacceptable to King Joseph.

While King Joseph and Marshal Jourdan favoured the 'wait and see' option, Marshal Victor pushed for the aggressive approach in battle that was favoured by Napoleon himself. The Emperor always felt that if the enemy army was in sight, it had to be attacked as soon as possible in order to destroy it at once. By waiting until the other French corps had arrived, the Anglo-Spanish army would probably have time to slip away and fight again another day. Marshal Victor wanted to attack as soon as possible. A few hours later, Col. Huguet-Châteaux was back at King Joseph's HQ asking for the support of Gen. Sébastiani's 4th Corps when Victor's 1st Corps attacked. Although both Joseph and Jourdan felt it was better to wait, they also knew that this would raise the wrath of their imperial master; they thus agreed to attack, except that 4th Corps would not be engaged until 1st Corps had captured the Cerro de Medellin from the British. This was the worst possible instruction considering that Wellesley had posted three brigades on the position.

Sleepless night

The British troops thus laid down, musket in hand hoping to get some kind of a night's sleep as, no doubt, did their Spanish comrades and also their French opponents. However, not all the French were sleepy and some of them would sneak up in small groups close to the allied line, rise up shouting, fire a volley in the air and run off in the darkness thus setting off the alarm. By the time everyone was up under arms, nothing was seen. In one case, the incident degenerated into an alarm with musketry fire followed by cannon shots, the British in the sector thinking they were under attack. At one in the morning, nervous Spanish gunners fired their cannons too at what turned out to be a stray cow.

Past midnight or one in the morning, more serious French troop movements could be perceived from the allied lines by the many torches moving about within the French lines. Much construction activity could also be heard on the Cerro de Cascajal. At about two in the morning, the moon brought its faint glow that revealed dark squares moving in the distance – French formations moving into their positions while artillery batteries were being built; there would surely be a battle the next day.

Like their British and Spanish counterparts, some French soldiers tried to go to sleep; those back from Marshal Victor's late attack had the added disadvantage of having damp uniforms from having crossed the Alberche and the Portina rivers on foot with nothing to replace them, since their baggage was further away. And the noise of the occasional shooting would stir anyone who managed to doze off in both camps. Finally, the thirsty from both sides would venture to get drinking water in the Portina's stream, often seeing other shadows doing the same thing on the nearby opposite bank. Nobody shot their muskets; indeed, some waved at each other in the night.

THE BATTLE CONTINUES, 28 JULY

As early dawn started lighting the area, men on either side now could see their opponents' formations better and better with each passing minute. Gathered in the area were nearly 100,000 fighting men, not counting non-combatants such as sutlers, servants and camp followers. There were at least 20,000 horses for cavalrymen, the artillery and supply trains. It was an imposing spectacle full of pageantry as the sun went up, showing the battalions and columns in their varied uniforms with their colours fluttering in the light morning breeze. The Anglo-Spanish army had the numerical advantage with some 52,200 men, but an estimated 32,000 were Spaniards whose battle performance could be uncertain for a variety of reasons. Some were unsteady as had been seen by the previous evening's panic. The 20,200 British troops present were certainly the better led, trained, disciplined and supplied soldiers of the allied army. But there were uncertainties for them too. Many had recently come from England and, from its generals to its privates, no British force had ever faced such a numerous French army whose commanders included two of Napoleon's marshals. On most of the field of Talavera that the British troops occupied, the ground was fairly flat so that Wellesley's usual practice of putting battalions behind slopes could not be implemented except in the Cerro de Medellin area. Most of the troops would thus have to face the effects of the French artillery.

The results of the noisy construction activity could be seen with imposing batteries now built with their guns ready to open fire. In terms of artillery, the French had the advantage with some 82 guns, many of which were 8- and 12-pdrs. The British had only 30 guns of smaller calibre, mainly 6-pdrs, which was a marked disadvantage. The Spanish had 30 guns of varied calibres and, presumably, ages although some would have been of the dependable Spanish version of the French Gribeauval system.

'All formation was lost, and each man fought for himself' at Talavera, 28 July 1809. At about three in the afternoon, Campbell's division managed to repulse the somewhat premature attack of Leval's division after a desperate fight. The British infantrymen are shown in the style of 1812. In 1809, they would have worn stovepipe shakos, white breeches and black knee gaiters. Print after C.B. (Private collection. Author's photo)

Lieutenant-General Wellesley and his staff went up to the secured Cerro de Medellin to have a better view of the future field of battle. The British officers soon saw a plumed cavalcade arriving at the back of the French lines. It was King Joseph and Marshal Jourdan with their staff officers and escorts. Marshal Victor was in the area of the Cerro de Cascajal with his corps getting ready to attack. General Sébastiani was further south, his corps facing the British troops above the Pajar de Vergara battery while Gen. Leval's troops, mostly allied German and Dutch units, faced the battery. Only Gen. Milhaud's dragoon division faced the Spanish army in the distance.

As can be seen, the disposition of the French army opposite the Anglo-Spanish army confirmed the French marshal's opinion, in that the one force to beat was Lt. Gen. Wellesley's British army. None of the French senior officers present had ever fought a British force in a full-scale battle. They had heard of the steadiness of British troops in battle from the previous campaigns in Portugal by Gen. Junot and Marshal Soult; the Corunna campaign had shown that the British could slip away to fight elsewhere. This time, the French hoped they would destroy the British army, which would spell doom for the Spanish patriot armies. Experience had shown that, brave as they might be, the Spanish could not hold their ground against French troops. After losing an entire army, Britain would likely withdraw what forces might be left in Portugal. At length, without British opposition, the imperial regime could be securely imposed on Spain and, ultimately, the whole Peninsula.

All this was not entirely wishful thinking. Most of the French army, if Victor's initial attack was successful, would concentrate on the smaller British contingent, which, if it broke and was overwhelmed, would not only provide a signal victory but end the Peninsular War. But, luckily for Lt. Gen. Wellesley, Marshal Victor was hampered by King Joseph and Marshal Jourdan while Gen. Sébastiani, although a corps commander, was somewhat neutral, being junior in rank. King Joseph was especially worried about the safety of Madrid. On their side Wellesley and Cuesta would stick to a defensive position. It was known that there were some French troop movements to the north-west, although there were no details so, for Wellesley, some caution was in order, while Cuesta dearly wished to liberate Madrid, but such a move could not be entertained unless Gen. Venegas's Spanish army of La Mancha was clearly known to be moving on Toledo and Madrid.

Morning attack

Marshal Victor's attack plan called for a diversion to be made on the small hills south of the Cerro de Medellin by Gen. Lapisse's division and Gen. Latour-Maubourg's cavalry, while Gen. Ruffin's division would make a frontal attack on the Cerro de Medellin, with the aim of taking it. General Villatte's division was in reserve behind the large battery on the Cerro de Cascajal. Gen. Ruffin's regiments went into action: the 9th Light Infantry opposite Stewart's brigade to the south, the 24th Line Infantry facing Tilson's brigade at the centre and the 96th Line Infantry at the north being the attacking force's reserve. The French had a numerical advantage of 4,900 men against 3,700. The only possible action was a frontal attack on the British position, but Marshal Victor underestimated the number of men necessary to carry the position. The odds would have been better if Villatte's 6,100 men had been added in immediate support or as the leading division, instead of Ruffin's already-mauled division.

On their side, the British troops could see the French preparations and they were ready to sustain the attack. Lieutenant-General Wellesley was on top of the Cerro de Medellin. It was about five in the morning. A cannon shot was fired from the large French battery on the Cerro de Cascajal; a few moments later, a tremendous detonation erupted as some 50 expertly served French guns opened fire sending a hail of cannonballs and shells on the British position targeted for the attack. The British had only 18 guns to oppose them at the Cerro de Medellin and it was a hopeless duel. Several British guns were put out of service and some of their ammunition boxes blew up. The French projectiles tore through many men in the British positions. Their officers allowed them to lie down to reduce the risk of being hit. Smoke was already starting to cover the field. After three-quarters of an hour, the French battery stopped firing.

Lines of French *voltigeurs* fanned out in front of their advancing regiments; the attack was on! For many young British soldiers this was their first battle experience; now they could hear the French drums rolling

Major-General Stapleton Cotton (later Lord Combermere). He was an experienced cavalry officer who had seen much service in India during the 1790s and, back in England, became major-general in 1805. In command of a brigade at Talavera, he went on to further distinction, especially at Salamanca in July 1812. He later served in the West Indies and in India, eventually becoming Constable of the Tower of London and field marshal. Print after Mary Martha Pearson. (Private collection. Author's photo)

and the shouts of '*Vive l'Empereur*' amidst the cannon shots. The French voices were getting nearer as their columns were increasingly seen through the smoke's haze. Quietly encouraged by their sergeants and veteran comrades, they remained steady and ready to meet the coming onslaught. The British forward skirmishers – riflemen of the 5th Battalion of the 60th – retreated to the main line while the French guns opened up again, this time at a longer range to hit troops further back and not their own men. The French 24th Line made good progress up the Cerro de Medellin having suffered only from the British riflemen's fire and some cannon shots. Major-General Hill was in command at that position and, when the 24th was about a 100m from the top, the men of six British battalions suddenly rose, appeared on top of the hill and aimed their muskets. Tremendous volleys erupted that took out entire ranks of French infantrymen; they stopped and tried to return the fire, but ineffectively as their formations were now disorderly. Hill now ordered a bayonet attack. The sight of the gleaming bayonets handled by screaming charging men broke what

The battle of Talavera, 28 July 1809. Print after R. Westhall. (Anne S.K. Brown Military Collection, Brown University Library, Providence. Author's photo)

formation was left and the French infantrymen ran down before they could be reached. The French 9th Light Infantry now came up and provided cover so that, according to Girod de l'Ain, the 24th could withdraw in order. Meanwhile, the French 96th Line Infantry was also coming up the Cerro de Medellin, but the 24th Line's rout exposed its southern flank. Lieutenant-General Sherbrooke had sent the King's German Legion's 5th Battalion to oppose the 96th and the Germans charged right into its exposed flank, causing some 400 casualties.

At that point, Wellesley ordered Brig. Gen. Stewart's brigade to make a bayonet charge on the routed French formations to finish them off. In so doing, many overenthusiastic British infantrymen ran right up to the narrow Portina River and some who were not out of breath crossed it and headed for the Cerro de Cascajal. They were soon cut down by the French guns and musket fire from Gen. Villatte's division. The surviving redcoats got back to their lines. The French artillery then opened fire again and kept it up for about an hour, after which it became silent again.

This first phase of the day's battle revealed to the British that their artillery was inadequate in calibre and in numbers for a major campaign against the French. There was also not enough cavalry. Had there been some at the Cerro de Medellin, it could have charged the fleeing French troops. The revelations were more sobering for the French who were somewhat amazed at the attack's failure. Their deployment and tactics usually provided them with battlefield successes, thanks to the psychological effect of their artillery barrages, their rolling drums and their war cries as they closed in. None of this had worked on the surprisingly resilient redcoats, whose murderous volley fire was very fearsome, especially when followed by bayonet attacks. The losses had been severe. Ruffin's division had some 1,300 casualties, while the British had lost about 750 men. And the battle had just started.

Truce and meeting

The hot Spanish sun was beaming down on the battlefield making putrid odours increasingly apparent. The bodies of the men slain on the previous night and at the morning's engagement were lying on the ground and slopes of the Cerro de Medellin and had to be buried right away. Both sides thus made a necessary truce to let parties of soldiers go and collect their dead to be thrown into the burial trenches that others were digging behind their respective lines; these would become the final and unmarked resting place of many a fine but unlucky man. It was about nine in the morning and, while some men were performing this gruesome task, many others in the French camp started cooking up their rations for a hurried snack. The British troops had no such luck since their food supplies had not come and some men, nearly starved, were reduced to foraging whatever seemed fit to eat, even if it came from haversacks of dead soldiers.

The men in both armies were also thirsty, especially as the hot Spanish sun was rising, and, profiting from the truce, approached the banks of the narrow Portina River, whose fresh, cool water flowed down from the northern hills. Thus, British and French soldiers found themselves filling their water canteens within a short distance of each other. This was the first time they came face to face not to kill each other and suspicion soon gave way to humane and cordial gestures on both sides. The stream was so narrow that some men shook hands, some helped fill the others' canteens while others joked and laughed.

Meanwhile, on the Cerro de Cascajal, the French senior officers had gathered for a high-level meeting. In attendance were marshals Jourdan and Victor, King Joseph and generals Sébastiani and Dessolle. The question was: the attack had failed so what next? Far from feeling defeated, Marshal Victor was adamant and urged that the attack be pressed on again, this time with the support of all other troops. The whole French line would advance. Two divisions of Sébastiani's corps would engage the British at the centre to keep them busy there while the rest of the force would attack the Cerro de Medellin again and this time, by sheer weight of numbers as well as by a flanking move northwards, the chances were deemed very good to carry the position and badly maul, if not destroy, the British army. As previously, Marshal Victor had no time for Spaniards; the British army was the one to beat and, by concentrating on it, the French enjoyed a two-to-one advantage. Victor was obviously sure that, as good as they seemed to be, the British would not be able to resist such an attack by Europe's best army.

Marshal Jourdan disagreed. In his view, it was better not to renew the action with another costly attack. It was wiser either to stay put on the east bank of the Portina or, even better in his mind, on the east bank of the

The battle of Talavera, 28 July 1809. Print after William Heath. (Anne S.K. Brown Military Collection, Brown University Library, Providence. Author's photo)

Albreche River that offered better defensive advantages. This, of course, did not sit very well with Victor and there were some tense exchanges. Jourdan's reasons to wait and see were quite good since his logic was based on Soult's troops coming down through Estramadura. He was expected within days and, with his arrival in the rear of the Anglo-Spanish army, the outcome was not in doubt. Victor, true to Napoleon's thinking, wanted to attack and destroy the enemy army before it could get away; he was sure that Wellesley and Cuesta would be warned by their scouts of Soult's impending arrival and slip away. Generals Sébastiani and Dessolle were more cautious and felt basically, like Jourdan, that it was better to wait for Soult and his 2nd Corps, especially since it was known that Ney's and Mortier's corps were also coming down. In all this, King Joseph had relatively different concerns; he was worried about the safety of Madrid and its surrounding area. Should the rumoured Spanish force operating somewhere south of Toledo march up, there might be an uprising in Madrid and that would be difficult to contain. It might mean that the army would have to march back to secure his capital. So he too sided with the cautious approach of Marshal Jourdan.

While these options were being discussed, a messenger arrived from Gen. Valence in Toledo; he announced that elements of the Spanish army of La Mancha under Gen. Venegas had appeared within sight of Toledo. General

Valence had only four Polish battalions to hold the city against over 20,000 opponents. They may have been Spaniards, but the odds were overwhelming all the same. This was very serious news because it confirmed King Joseph's worst fears and vindicated Marshal Jourdan's caution. Hardly had this news arrived than another rider appeared at full gallop. It was one of Marshal Soult's aides-de-camp and he too had some very sobering new developments to relay. Soult was delayed by several days owing to the difficulty his artillery had had travelling down while Marshal Ney's supporting 6th Corps was also suffering delays. At best, Marshal Soult's 2nd Corps would not reach Plasencia before 3 August with Ney's 6th Corps and Mortier's 5th Corps in the following days.

The situation had suddenly changed. It would take at least a week until pressure could be brought on the rear of the Anglo-Spanish army. Instead of squeezing Wellesley and Cuesta, the French were now looking at the prospect of being outflanked in the east with Madrid and Toledo in jeopardy. King Joseph and Marshal Jourdan simply had to bring Gen. Sébastiani's 4th Corps back east to deal with this new threat. This would leave Marshal Victor and his 1st Corps outnumbered in front of the Anglo-Spanish army at Talavera. For Victor, all this pointed to the only option: attack now! Beat Wellesley and Cuesta today and then deal with Venegas. King Joseph and Marshal Jourdan agreed. The battle would go on.

The 48th Foot and Lt. Col. Charles Donnellan at Talavera, 28 July 1809. As the 48th advanced into battle, Donnellan had two horses shot from under him until he was very gravely wounded. This print after Ernest Ibbetson shows the moment when, wounded, he passed the command to Major Middlemore telling him that he 'would have the honour of leading the 48th to the charge'. Although powdered hair and queues had been abolished since August 1808, Donnellan continued to wear this fashion to his death. (Private collection. Author's photo)

Renewed attacks

On top of the Cerro de Medellin, Wellesley and his staff were noting the increased activity in the French camp. French generals and their own staff officers were galloping back to their divisions that now stirred again as soldiers went back to their lines. The truce was obviously coming to an end and there would be another French attack. There was little doubt in Wellesley's mind that, once again, the French would ignore the Spanish and concentrate on his British contingent. Taking into account the previous attacks and the topography of the area, he had made adjustments to his army's positions. The first most obvious move the French might make would be to outflank the Cerro de Medellin and take possession of the Northern Plain. To prevent this, Anson's and Fane's cavalry brigades were posted on the western end of the plain and Rettberg's battery of the King's German Legion artillery was posted on the northern slopes of the Cerro de Medellin to cover whatever might appear on the plain. General Cuesta agreed that this was most likely where the next attack would occur and, at Wellesley's behest, detached Gen. Bassecourt's reserve division of some 5,000 men to be posted

Death of Lt. Col. Charles Donnellan of 48th Foot, Talavera, 28 July 1809. Now on the ground in his last moments, urging his regiment on. Print after Paul Hardy. (Private collection. Author's photo)

on the southern slopes of the Sierra de Segurilla in order to cover completely the access to the Northern Plain. He also detached the Duke of Albuquerque's cavalry to support the British cavalry and sent a few guns to reinforce Rettberg's battery. The northern flank of the Anglo-Spanish army was thus secure from a French surprise attack.

This was indeed partly what the French intended. Shunning a frontal attack on the Cerro de Medellin, since the previous ones had been repulsed with many casualties, the French generals decided to send a substantial force north of the Cerro de Medellin to enter the Northern Plain. They expected the British would be watching and sending more troops there to secure the area. But it would be a feint attack. The real assault would come from Gen. Sébastiani's 4th Corps, the men of which had not yet been engaged. They would charge into the British line north of the allied battery at Pagar de Vergara. Latour-Maubourg's dragoons would be behind 4th Corps, ready to charge if the British line broke. General Lapisse's division of the 1st Corps would face the King's German Legion's battalion and 83rd Foot and, if it also broke through, would assault the Cerro de Medellin. According to this plan, the British army would then be pierced and, if the diversion from the north worked, squeezed between two French contingents.

To keep the Spanish preoccupied, Gen. Leval's division of German and Dutch battalions would attack the Pajar de Vergara area and Gen. Milhaud's cavalry was to cover the Spanish further south outside Talavera. Light infantryman Girod de l'Ain, who had survived the previous actions, was happy that his mauled unit was not deployed for another attack and spent

The battle of Talavera, 28 July 1809. Another impression of the engagement shown in this print after William Heath. (Anne S.K. Brown Military Collection, Brown University Library, Providence. Author's photo)

Note: Gridlines are shown at intervals of 1km

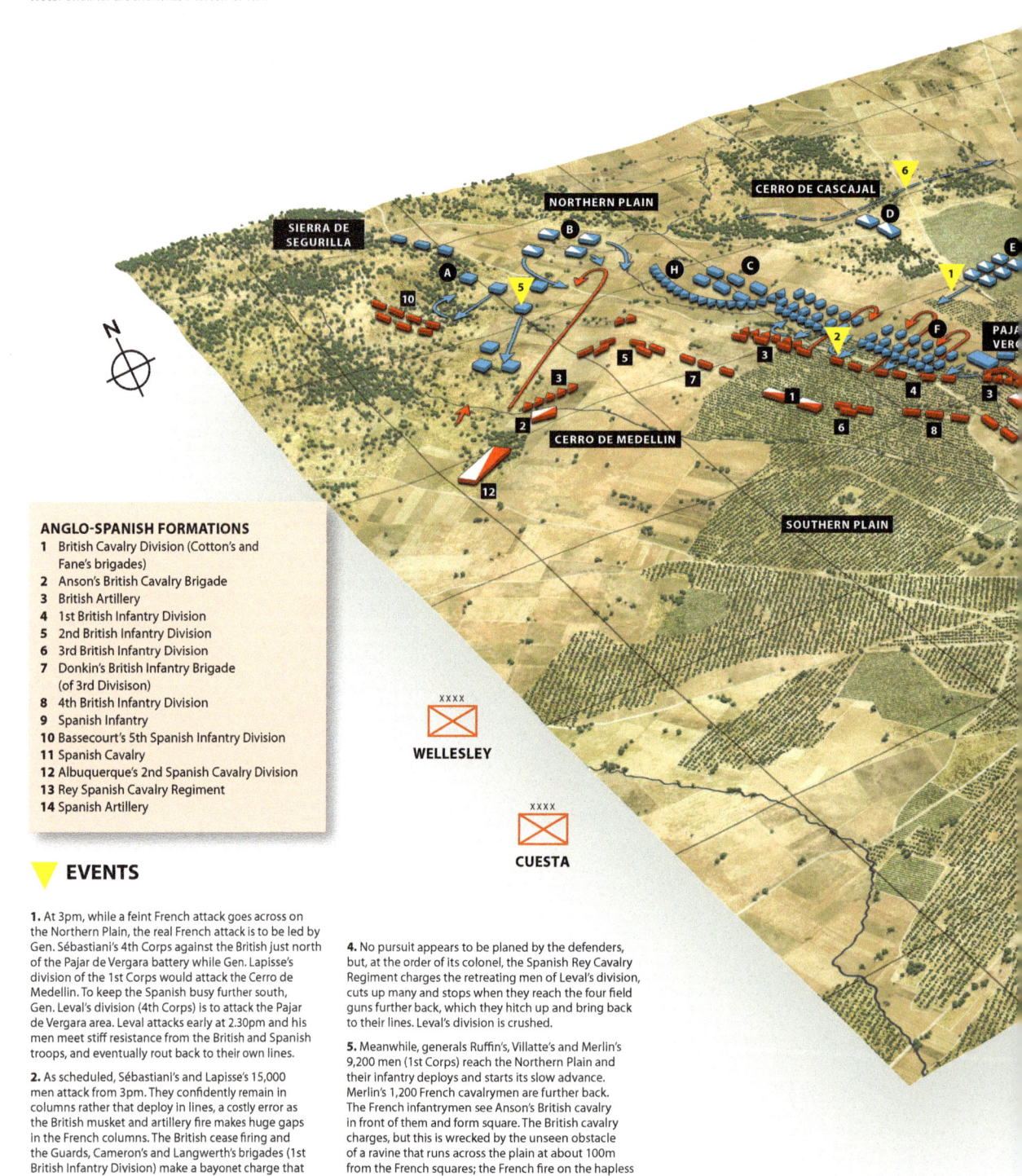

ANGLO-SPANISH FORMATIONS
1. British Cavalry Division (Cotton's and Fane's brigades)
2. Anson's British Cavalry Brigade
3. British Artillery
4. 1st British Infantry Division
5. 2nd British Infantry Division
6. 3rd British Infantry Division
7. Donkin's British Infantry Brigade (of 3rd Division)
8. 4th British Infantry Division
9. Spanish Infantry
10. Bassecourt's 5th Spanish Infantry Division
11. Spanish Cavalry
12. Albuquerque's 2nd Spanish Cavalry Division
13. Rey Spanish Cavalry Regiment
14. Spanish Artillery

▼ EVENTS

1. At 3pm, while a feint French attack goes across on the Northern Plain, the real French attack is to be led by Gen. Sébastiani's 4th Corps against the British just north of the Pajar de Vergara battery while Gen. Lapisse's division of the 1st Corps would attack the Cerro de Medellin. To keep the Spanish busy further south, Gen. Leval's division (4th Corps) is to attack the Pajar de Vergara area. Leval attacks early at 2.30pm and his men meet stiff resistance from the British and Spanish troops, and eventually rout back to their own lines.

2. As scheduled, Sébastiani's and Lapisse's 15,000 men attack from 3pm. They confidently remain in columns rather that deploy in lines, a costly error as the British musket and artillery fire makes huge gaps in the French columns. The British cease firing and the Guards, Cameron's and Langwerth's brigades (1st British Infantry Division) make a bayonet charge that overreaches itself and they in turn are badly mauled by a French counterattack. This is checked by Wellesley who sends additional troops from Mackenzie's 2nd Division to cover the retreating redcoats.

3. At 4pm, Gen. Leval's division (4th Corps) attacks the Pajar de Vergara battery. The place has been reinforced by more Spanish troops and the French come up against a withering fire and, once again, the attacking force wavers and starts a fairly orderly retreat.

4. No pursuit appears to be planed by the defenders, but, at the order of its colonel, the Spanish Rey Cavalry Regiment charges the retreating men of Leval's division, cuts up many and stops when they reach the four field guns further back, which they hitch up and bring back to their lines. Leval's division is crushed.

5. Meanwhile, generals Ruffin's, Villatte's and Merlin's 9,200 men (1st Corps) reach the Northern Plain and their infantry deploys and starts its slow advance. Merlin's 1,200 French cavalrymen are further back. The French infantrymen see Anson's British cavalry in front of them and form square. The British cavalry charges, but this is wrecked by the unseen obstacle of a ravine that runs across the plain at about 100m from the French squares; the French fire on the hapless horsemen. Some are rallied by Lt. Col. Elley who manages to charge on further east with about 180 men. He is met by Merlin's 1,200 French troopers and few British cavalrymen escape.

6. By 5pm, generals Ruffin and Villatte learn that the other attacks have failed. They order a withdrawal back to the Cerro de Cascajal signalling the end of the battle. During the evening, the whole French army retreats to the east bank of the Albreche River.

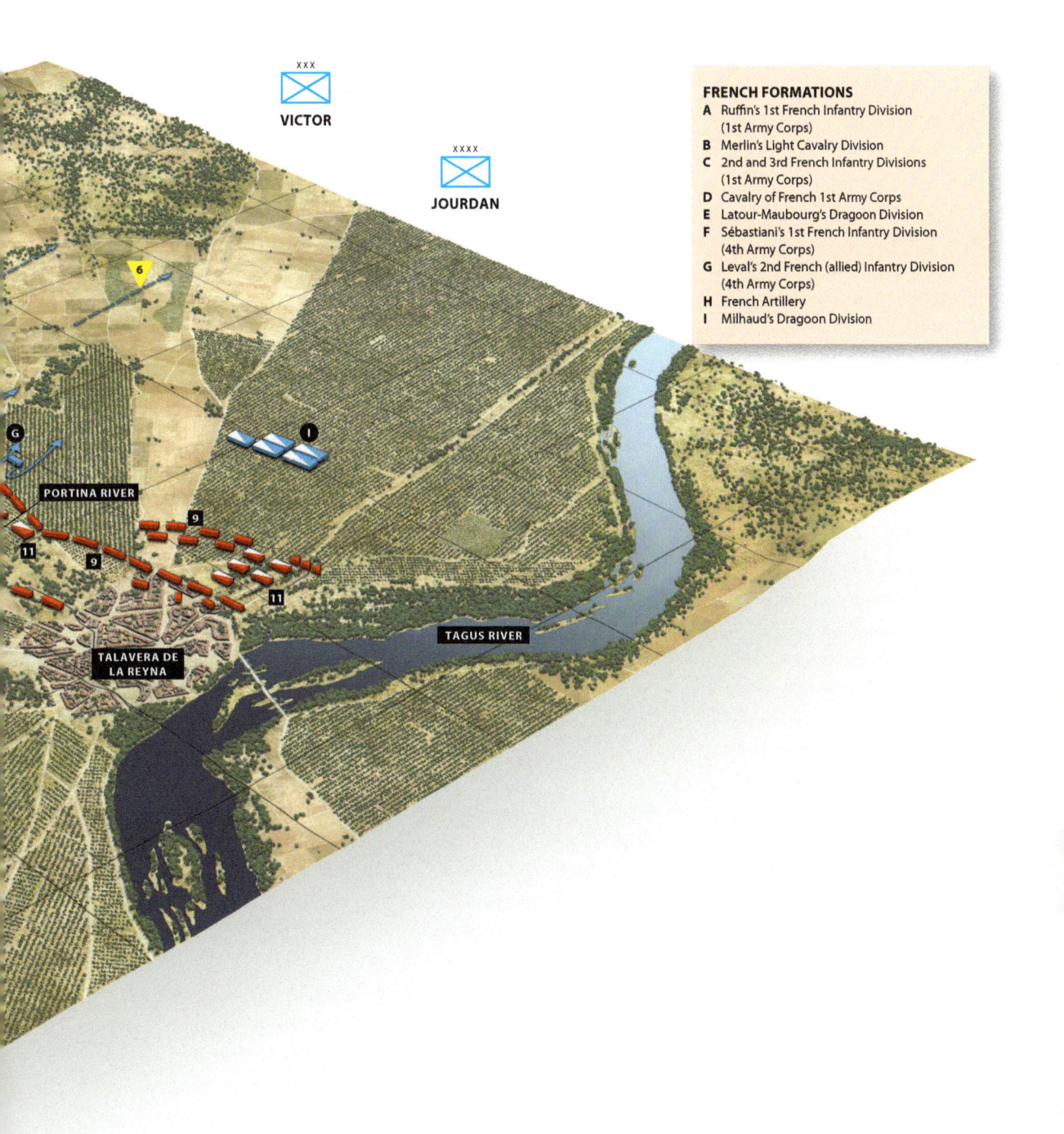

FRENCH FORMATIONS
- **A** Ruffin's 1st French Infantry Division (1st Army Corps)
- **B** Merlin's Light Cavalry Division
- **C** 2nd and 3rd French Infantry Divisions (1st Army Corps)
- **D** Cavalry of French 1st Army Corps
- **E** Latour-Maubourg's Dragoon Division
- **F** Sébastiani's 1st French Infantry Division (4th Army Corps)
- **G** Leval's 2nd French (allied) Infantry Division (4th Army Corps)
- **H** French Artillery
- **I** Milhaud's Dragoon Division

TALAVERA, AFTERNOON OF 28 JULY 1809

The morning of 28 July finds the Anglo-Spanish army solidly disposed from the Tagus River northwards to the slopes of the mountainous Sierra de Segurilla, which makes a surprise flank attack by the enemy almost impossible. Except for King Joseph's reserve kept much further eastwards, the whole French army is now on the east side of the river. The only way to destroy the Anglo-Spanish army, Marshal Victor argues, is to attack and crush it right away. An initial morning attack is soon routed by the British. King Joseph and Marshal Jourdan hesitate, but let Victor have it his way. A massive attack by both French corps is to be launched on the British positions at three in the afternoon.

'the rest of the day on the height to the right [the Cerro de Cascajal] from where we dominated the whole battlefield and could, as in front-row seats, follow all its incidents.'

Sure enough, at about two in the afternoon, the 30 guns of the large French battery on the Cerro de Cascajal opened – the truce was definitely over. The French cannonballs were mostly aimed at the British positions, hoping to soften them up before the attack. The allied artillery's inferiority, both in numbers and calibres, meant that little could be done other than take cover as best as one could; its guns would be used most efficiently on the French battalions when they attacked.

The French attack was set to start at three. Events were to decide otherwise. A nervous Gen. Leval, who was to engage his troops later, actually sent them into battle half an hour earlier. His advancing men, who had been deployed in a single line, at once encountered difficulties because of vineyards, stone fences and olive groves that upset the order of the advancing line and hampered visibility. This last factor meant that his division's artillery could not distinguish friend from foe and so had to remain silent. Nevertheless, the Nassau Regiment progressed, came upon British outposts and then went on towards the infantrymen of Campbell's division shouting '*Viva los Ingleses!*' (Long live the English!) to pass for Spanish troops. This trick initially worked,

The 3rd Foot Guards repulsing the French attack on the centre of the position at Talavera and about to make a bayonet charge, 28 July 1809. Print after Cecil C.P. Lawson. (Anne S.K. Brown Military Collection, Brown University Library, Providence. Author's photo)

the British officers instructing their men to hold their fire. The Baden and Dutch troops were meanwhile getting closer to the ten-cannon Pajar de Vergara battery, upon which Leval's gunners opened fire, finally having found a clear bearing. Leval's advance, which had gone quite well so far, was now about to meet some opposition. The 2nd Battalion of 24th Foot was lined up between Campbell's and the Guards brigade and it delivered deadly volleys on the north flank of the Nassau Regiment as it deployed; it was too much for its men and they withdrew. The Pajar de Vergara battery opened up on the Baden troops at close range, which killed Col. von Porbeck with many of his men. Seeing the enemy troops wavering, Lt. Col. Myers holding a colour and leading on foot, now conducted a counter-attack with the 7th, 40th and 53rd British regiments. Leval's soldiers broke and ran, hotly pursued by British troops who soon reached six of Leval's field guns that were quickly captured. There was no time to bring them back so they were immediately spiked. Briadier-General Campbell did not wish his men to go too far and ordered them back. The Dutch, Baden and Nassau battalions were in full retreat. The Hesse-Darmstadt and Frankfurt battalions had meantime engaged Spanish troops further south; they now saw the rest of their division running back and thus also broke action and retreated, but in an orderly fashion. Up on the Cerro de Medellin, a delighted Wellesley sent his compliments to Campbell. General Leval lost up to 700 men, most of them from Baden, in three-quarters of an hour's fighting. But he was not one to feel beaten and was busy rallying his troops.

By now, the temperature was some 40 degrees Celsius and the soldiers about to go into the next phase of the battle were sweating in their uniforms. At about three, as scheduled, the infantry divisions led by generals Lapisse and Sébastiani in person started moving in columns towards the British lines. It was a sizeable force of over 15,000 men moving in 12 attack columns followed by another 12 supporting columns. Further back stood over 3,000 cavalrymen ready to charge on broken enemy lines. Some two-dozen divisional field guns added their fire to those on the Cerro de Cascajal. It provided an extraordinary view of deadly pageantry with colours fluttering and gleaming bayonets of compact masses of men in uniform marching. When they got to the Portina River, which was just an easily crossed stream at that point, the French guns fell silent. Looking down from their lookout on the hill, the French marshals and generals were confident that, this time, the British would be overwhelmed by the strength of this attack, as had so many other enemy armies across Europe before this day.

They had reason to be confident since the British force that their columns were coming up against numbered some 8,000 men, a two-to-one advantage for the French. The French field officers were so confident they would break the British, they did not feel it necessary to deploy their battalions into lines; the columns would ram through the redcoats. It proved to be a costly mistake. The British line was in two ranks and Lt. Gen. Sherbrooke gave the order not to fire until the French were within only 50m. The British field batteries in the sector were shooting grapeshot at the advancing columns who, when they reached the fateful 50m, received musket volleys fired rapidly and with precision. Great gaps appeared in the columns as scores of men fell. Being in columns, the French infantrymen could not return fire as effectively at the British as if they had been in line. The surviving French soldiers in the front of the columns were dazed and awed.

At that point, the British line stopped firing. Bayonets were already fixed and, as ordered, the British infantrymen charged. The moment was perfect: the French, recalled Chambray, had lost the will to attack and stood 'in disorderly and cleared ranks', their 'surprise caused by the enemy's unexpected charge' spread dismay; 'we had to flee.' The Guards brigade had been the most eager to charge and had not even fired its muskets when it ran towards the French, followed by the 61st, 83rd and the King's German Legion battalions. This time, some French units proved more resilient. What happened to the 83rd Foot was recorded by Col. Vigo-Roussillon commanding the French 8th Line Regiment:

> A column of infantry [the 83rd Foot] was coming towards my battalion… I let them approach as much as they wanted. My soldiers … were ready, I had absolutely forbidden any firing before I would give the order and instructed that it would be battalion volley firing. When this column was about 60 paces away, I saw its chief become agitated; he did not know how to get out of the bad position he had engaged in… At the moment when he ordered his men to turn back, I ordered 'Battalion Fire!' No shot was wasted. The whole front of the 83rd [British] Infantry went down.

A detachment of the 2nd Dutch Regiment skirmishing in Spain, c.1808–1809. This unit was part of Gen. Leval's 2nd Division in the 4th Corps. Dutch infantry wore white uniforms with various facings for the regiments, the 2nd having sky blue and the 4th a light crimson hue. Print after J. Hoynck Van Papendrecht. (Private collection. Author's photo)

The 83rd Foot lost 283 men that day. Lieutenant-Colonel Gordon, surely the 'chief' seen by Vigo-Roussillon, was amongst the 42 killed. The 61st also suffered heavy casualties. The charge of the British regiments was getting out of control and the situation was becoming critical. Brigadier-General Cameron managed to stop his units, the 61st and what was left of the 83rd, from crossing the Portina, but the Guards and the King's German Legion kept on going, blinded by courageous battle rage to reach the French second column. They were going too far; as they ran, they became an easy target for the French. The Guards were now suffering increasingly high casualties from a French battery firing on their flank. A party of the King's German Legion that made it as far as the foot of the Cerro de Cascajal now found itself assailed on all sides and Brig. Gen. Langwerth was killed trying to rally his men to withdraw. Further south, the Guards were badly mauled by the sabre cuts of two regiments of Latour-Maubourg's dragoons. The guardsmen at last came to their senses and started to withdraw slowly and in good order.

Thus, remnants of British battalions were going back to assume their original positions on the west bank of the Portina, but they were much weakened and certainly somewhat dispirited. The French saw their chance finally to break the British line and still had many fresh units to attempt it. Up on the Cerro de Medellin, Lt. Gen. Wellesley had observed everything with the greatest calm. He foresaw that the French would exploit the weakened British position and ordered reinforcements to move up. The 2nd Battalion of the 24th and 1st Battalion of the 48th were called upon to cover the Guards' and the King's German Legion's withdrawal while Maj. Gen. Mackenzie advanced the 1st Battalion of the 31st and 2nd Battalion of the 45th to occupy the original position held by the Guards. Cotton's cavalry also moved closer as did two Spanish battalions. Thus, when the French 32nd and 75th Line Infantry Regiments attacked, they were coming up against an already-reinforced British front. Indeed, the 48th advanced into battle better to cover the retreat of many men of the King's German Legion who were being hemmed in by the French 8th and 54th of the Line under Gen. Lapisse. In spite of French artillery fire, the British 48th Foot advanced steadily. Coming under heavy fire, Lt. Col. Donellan of the 48th was seriously wounded and passed command over to Maj. Middlemore who engaged the French infantrymen. The British volleys hit many French soldiers including Gen. Lapisse who suffered a mortal wound. At this news, some of his men lost heart and retreated to the foot of the Cerro de Cascajal. Seeing this, Marshal Victor rushed down amongst the men to rally them. By then, the 48th had retreated to its position on the west side of the Portina. The main French attack had failed.

Yet another attempt
General Leval had meanwhile regrouped his division and was determined to mount another attack on the Pajar de Vergara battery. At about four in the afternoon, the division moved again on its target. This time, the British were not about to be distracted by tricks to confuse them. Furthermore, two Spanish battalions had joined them. Spanish cavalry was also nearby, ready to charge if given the opportunity. As Leval's battalions charged in another all-out frontal attack they came up against a withering fire and many a brave soldier fell without having a chance to inflict injuries to the enemy; such punishment could not be sustained for long and, once again, the attacking force wavered and started a fairly orderly retreat.

Observing this at the head of his regiment, Col. José de Lastres saw the opportunity, turned to his troopers of the Spanish El Rey Regiment and ordered the charge. No doubt unexpected by Leval's men, the charging troopers galloped upon them, reaching the flank of their retreating battalions. The German infantrymen had no time to form a defence line. The shock was severe and devastating, the Spaniard's sabres swinging and cutting soon transformed the once-orderly retreat into a near-panic rout. Whatever shooting

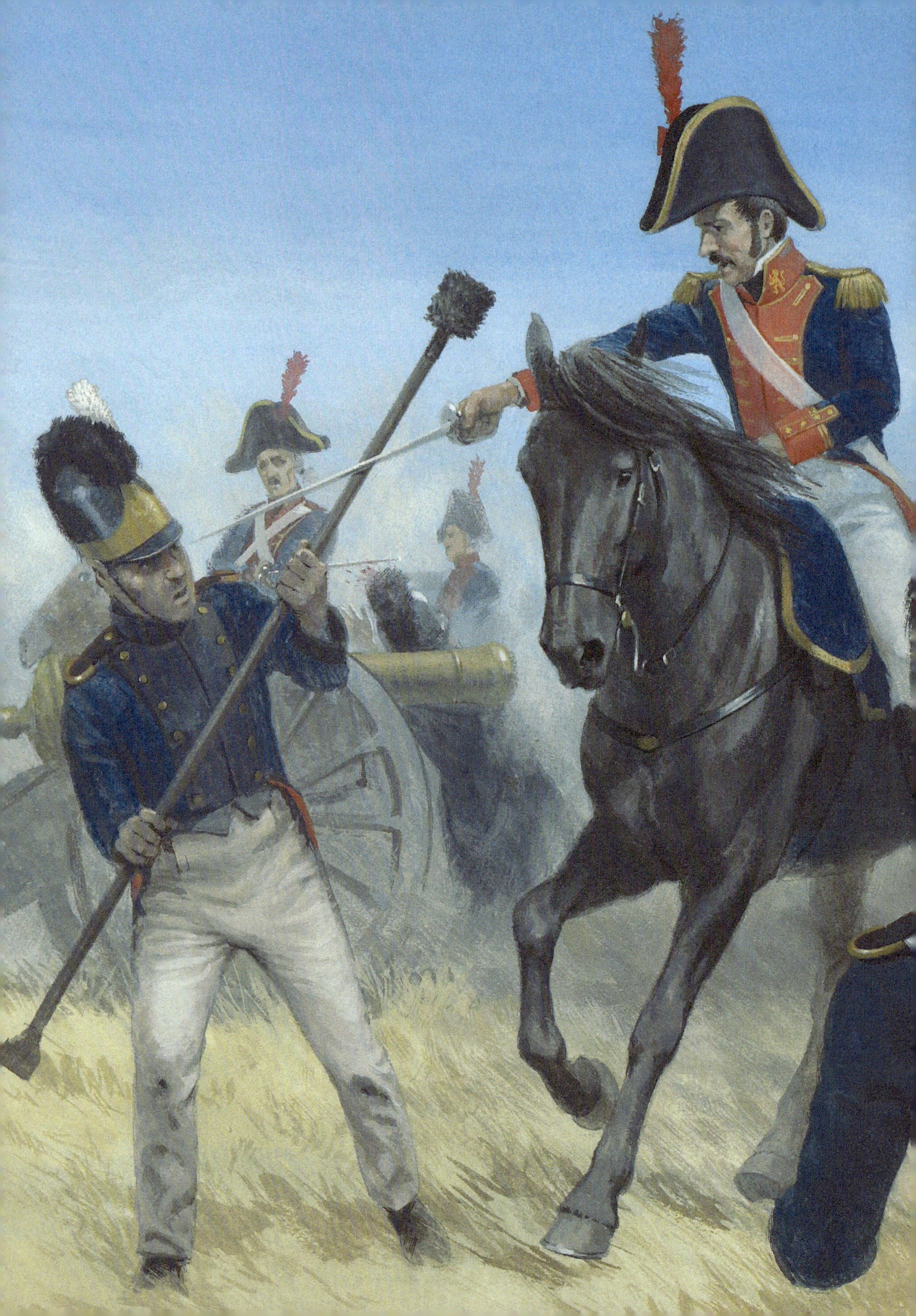

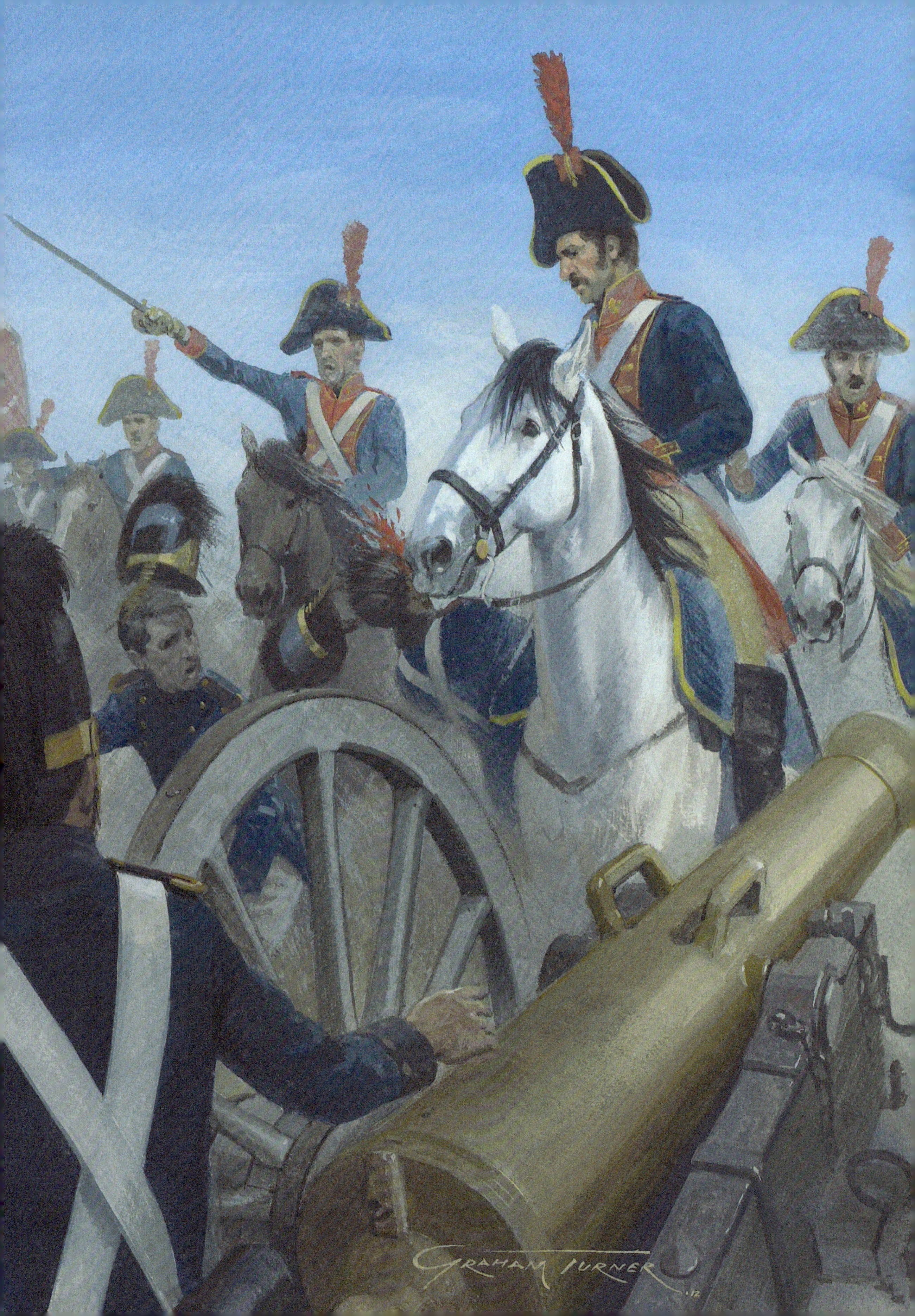
GRAHAM TURNER

THE CHARGE OF THE SPANISH CAVALRY REGIMENT EL REY (PP. 70–71)

At about four in the afternoon of 28 July, Gen. Leval's German battalions of Hesse-Darmstadt, Baden and Frankfurt made a second attempt to drive British and Spanish troops holding Pajar de Vergara. They were greeted by heavy fire from the British line that stopped them. The Spanish Cavalry Regiment El Rey **(1)** was nearby and then charged Leval's battalions. General Cuesta, in his after-report on 7 August 1809, paid particular tribute to the Cavalry Regiment El Rey (the King's) for its 'intrepid attack and destruction of a column of enemy infantry. Its colonel, Don José Maria de Lastra, was wounded during the charge and was succeeded with valour by Lt. Col. Don Rafael Valparda. Capt. Don Francisco de Sierra gained much distinction by taking a cannon while vanquishing its defenders; Ensign Don Pablo Cataneo, of 16 years of age, slew four Frenchmen, and all officers and men of the regiment manifested proof of its valour and discipline.' Indeed, the regiment did very well since, besides the gun taken by Capt-Sierra, three more were taken (in all three from the Baden **(2)** and one from the Hessian contingents) by the Cavalry Regiment El Rey in this obviously perfectly executed charge that caught Leval's Hessian and Frankfurt lines of troops on their flank and hacked them to pieces until the survivors managed to form two squares and withdraw. The valiant charge of the Cavalry Regiment El Rey put an end to Leval's attacks that completely failed.

LEFT
Corporal of *voltigeurs*, Hessian Crown Prince Regiment, 1808–1813. The Hesse contingent was part of General Leval's 2nd Division. Watercolour by Pierre Albert Leroux. (Anne S.K. Brown Military Collection, Brown University Library, Providence. Author's photo)

RIGHT
Senior NCO, 1st Light Dragoons, King's German Legion. It was part of Anson's cavalry brigade at Talavera. The uniform shown in this 1814–1815 print by Martinet was worn by this unit from 1807. (Anne S.K. Brown Military Collection, Brown University Library, Providence. Author's photo)

Leval's soldiers might have directed at the El Rey Regiment was inadequate. The blue-coated heavy cavalrymen galloped on and came upon four enemy field guns further back. The Spanish troopers quickly vanquished their Baden and Hessian gunners and, halting their charge, now brought the guns back. The surviving Hessian and Frankfurt infantrymen had meanwhile managed to form themselves in two squares. The fighting in this part of the field was over.

This charge, which turned out to be the final blow that crushed the attacks of Leval's division, illustrates that the Spanish troops, while often as useless as their French enemies and British allies thought they were, could nevertheless surprise everyone with a startling blow. The Spanish army of the Peninsular War lacked everything except courage and tenacity. As often noted by observers, some of its units were of rather doubtful value facing French imperial troops, but others could stand against the enemy very well. Such a unit was the El Rey Regiment. It was a proud old unit whose origins went back to 1538, the oldest lineage for a Spanish cavalry regiment, and it bore the title 'The King's' (El Rey in Spanish). Many of its officers and men were veterans of the old pre-1808 army in a senior regiment that must have been much better trained and appointed than the more recent units. Thus this surprise to the French from the Spanish basically stopped the French from further attempts on the southern part of the battlefield.

The northern sector
Meanwhile, the great French artillery battery on the Cerro de Cascajal had relentlessly pounded the British troops on the Cerro de Medellin during the afternoon and this caused a good many casualties amongst the redcoats. For instance, Col. Donkin's brigade had lost nearly 200 men without being even engaged in battle. In spite of the inferiority in number and calibre of its guns, the British artillery in the area managed to aim shots that tore through some lines of Gen. Villatte's troops on the Cerro de Cascajal.

Fusilier private, Baden Infantry Regiment, *c.*1809–1812. This regiment, part of Gen. Leval's 2nd Division in 4th Corps, was heavily engaged at Talavera on 28 July. Watercolour by Pierre Albert Leroux. (Anne S.K. Brown Military Collection, Brown University Library, Providence. Author's photo)

Wellesley and his staff on top of the Cerro de Medellin observed increasing movements by the French troops opposite them. They were, by the thousands, moving further north and it soon became clear that their purpose was to outflank the Anglo-Spanish army by taking the Northern Plain. To do so, some 8,000 infantrymen from Gen. Ruffin's and Villatte's divisions from 1st Corps would attack the allied troops there with the support of Gen. Merlin's 1,200 cavalrymen from 4th Corps. It was Marshal Victor's latest gamble finally to break the allied line and, if all went well, charge down on the flank of Wellesley's and Cuesta's troops and destroy both armies.

It will be recalled that Lt. Gen. Wellesley had posted troops there earlier since he had learned fast that the wily French marshal could offer some nasty surprises. General Bassecourt's Spanish infantry division guarded the northern flank of the Northern Plain, the plain itself had Fane and Anson's cavalry brigades with the Duke of Albuquerque's cavalry division behind them. The duke, who did not think much of Cuesta, was very displeased at being posted there. The northern slopes of the Cerro de Medellin held Spanish and King's German Legion artillery batteries and Brig. Gen. Stewart's infantry brigade. The British troops made up about 4,000 men, a number that was about doubled by the presence of the Spanish troops although, as will be seen, they were not all deployed.

The French advanced, with the seasoned 9th Light Infantry on their northern flank skirting the slopes of the Sierra de Segurilla with a fan of *voltigeurs* in front, heading west towards Gen. Bassecourt's Spanish division that had about eight battalions. The rest of the French force advanced covering the width of the Northern Plain, Gen. Ruffin's division being next to the 9th Light Infantry with the 24th Line Infantry, 96th Line Infantry and Gen. Villatte's 27th Light Infantry to the south of the plain. The 63rd Line Infantry and a composite grenadier battalion were behind at the centre forming the reserve. Since each regiment had three battalions, the French infantry moving westward would have numbered 19 battalions, a respectable total. Further behind was a mixed and colourful cavalcade made up of four squadrons of the elite Polish Vistula Legion lancers, two squadrons of German Westphalian Light Horse and five squadrons from 10th and 26th Regiments of Chasseurs à cheval.

As they advanced, the French were very cautious and thus progressed rather slowly. They now perceived that a large body of British cavalry was in front of them about a kilometre away and that it seemed about to charge them. The French formations now formed squares in order to be able to repel the horsemen better. In doing so, their formations became more concentrated, which the Spanish and German Legion gunners on the Cerro de Medellin noted with satisfaction as infantry squares made ideal targets. A party of French *voltigeurs* started up the slopes of the Cerro de Medellin but were soon driven off by British skirmishers.

The French had thus stopped their advance, certainly trying to fathom just how much opposition was in front of them when, on the British side, trumpets sounded and the cavalry advanced in two lines with the obvious intention of charging. Sure enough, the charge had been ordered and the cavalrymen trotted up: 23rd Light Dragoons heading for the large square of 27th Light Infantry, 1st King's German Legion Hussars going for the smaller squares of 24th and 96th Line Infantry. As they advanced faster and faster, sabres high, the attacking troopers came upon an unseen and unexpected obstacle hidden by the long grass: a ravine that ran across the plain at about a 100m from the French squares. It seems the French had not seen this ravine either, into the bed of which the waters from the Sierra flowed in the early

Officer and troopers of the Polish Vistula Legion, *c.*1809–1811. These lancers were engaged in the action on the Northern Plain that nearly destroyed the British 23rd Light Dragoons. Print after Sorieul. (Anne S.K. Brown Military Collection, Brown University Library, Providence. Author's photo)

Battle of Talavera, 28 July 1809, northern sector

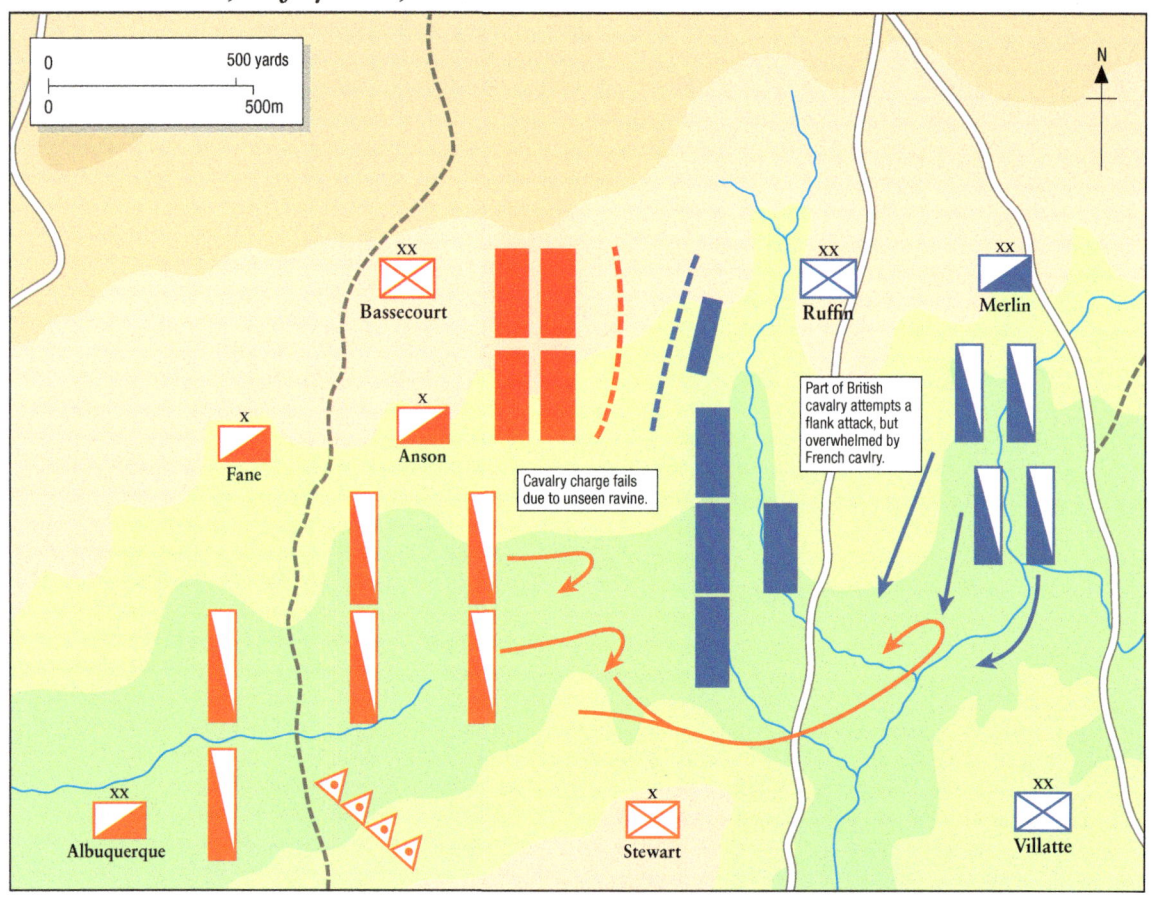

spring and which was now, in July, bone dry and rocky. It was about 2–2.5m deep and 3.5–5m wide. The first line of the charging cavalrymen saw it too late and many tumbled into it, the troopers often being thrown, some horses falling down and, if not injured, climbing out and running in all directions on the field. Lieutenant-Colonel Elley of the 23rd Light Dragoons managed to jump over the ravine since he was riding a thoroughbred horse, but ordinary cavalry horses could not match this feat. This chaos, which raised clouds of dust, was compounded when part of the second line of charging light dragoon troopers ran into the gully; the second line of King's German Legion hussars just narrowly missed it and stopped. The charge was totally ruined. The French perceived something had gone wrong, did not wonder long what had occurred and simply opened fire on whatever was out there.

In spite of all this, the officers rallied the men that were still mounted. These were mostly from the second line and they tried to attack the French squares, but the infantrymen's volleys made the British troopers turn back. However, a group of about 170 troopers of the 23rd Light Dragoons led by Lt. Col. Elley galloped ahead, passing by the square of the 27th Light Infantry and rode eastwards, perhaps hoping to create a flanking movement. Unfortunately for them, their initiative ran into the cavalrymen of 10th and 27th Chasseurs à cheval followed by the Vistula Legion lancers and the Westphalian Light Horse. Instead of fighting, the 10th Chasseurs à cheval fanned out letting the British troopers charge on and then closed in behind them. Thus, the British now had to face the Vistula Lancers and the Westphalians charging their front while the Chasseurs à cheval attacked their rear and sides. At odds of at least seven to one in favour of the French, the resulting action was fierce but the British troopers were soon overwhelmed, many were slain, more surrendered and, rather miraculously, Lt. Col. Elley managed to escape back with a few light dragoons to the Spanish lines held by Bassecourt's division on the slopes of the sierra. Elley must have blessed his luck and his investment in a thoroughbred horse. But his regiment had lost nearly 200 men and over 220 horses.

In his *History of the War in the Peninsula*, Napier mentioned an anecdote from Col. Rufane Donkin, who then commanded a brigade, which relates to an incident 'just as the French were coming on to the final attack'. This must have been at the outset of the British charge. A 'Spanish officer in a yellow [dragoon] uniform, with silver epaulettes, rode up' towards Gen. Wellesley and his staff. It was an aide-de-camp from the Duke of Albuquerque and he told Col. Rufane Donkin, that 'I am sent by the Duke of Albuquerque to desire that Sir Arthur Wellesley may be informed that the Spanish General will afford him no assistance in this battle, and that he is in communication with the enemy.' Donkin thus went to Wellesley bearing this message, which he received without the least 'sign of surprise' and simply answered 'Oh, very well, you may go back to your brigade!' Wellesley later said he had no recollection of the incident, but Donkin most certainly did and was impressed by 'his look, the calm manner in which he turned himself back again to view the battle.' Assuming it did occur, and there is no reason to put forward to explain why Donkin would invent such a tale, it would seem that when the Duke of Albuquerque saw the fiasco of the British cavalry in front of him, he made sure he would not be part of it. It will be recalled that the duke and Gen. Cuesta were not on the best of terms. It gives an insight into the bitter political atmosphere that was rampant in the Spanish senior staff at the time.

All this action on the Northern Plain was going on at about the same time as the previously described attack and repulse of Gen. Leval's renewed assault on the centre of the Anglo-Spanish line. Eventually, on the Northern Plain, generals Ruffin and Villatte learned that the action by Gen. Leval's troops further south had slackened and, eventually, stopped; there was no point in advancing further on the Northern Plain. It was now about five in the afternoon and the battle was essentially over. The retreat of Ruffin's and Villatte's troops back to the Cerro de Cascajal was sounded.

Private, 3rd Foot Guards, c.1809. As can be seen, he has reversed arms in a graveyard, an obvious sober reminder of the human cost of war. Talavera turned out to be one of the bloodiest battles of the Peninsular War. Watercolour by J. Atkinson. (Anne S.K. Brown Military Collection, Brown University Library, Providence. Author's photo)

Wellesley did not wish to follow the retreating French; that would have meant an assault on the Cerro de Cascajal and his troops were in no condition to attempt such an attack. Quite apart from not having been supplied for many days with food, as originally agreed by the Spanish, his men were exhausted and quite a few were missing from the roll calls. Nor did he encourage any initiative from the Spanish troops. Some units were very good, but most of them were not sufficiently disciplined, were badly armed, largely underfed and poorly led. There was also the Spanish generals' bickering. Perhaps for all these reasons, Cuesta attempted nothing further.

Marshal Victor was not yet discouraged in spite of the successive failure of all the French attacks, and he sent word to King Joseph and Marshal Jourdan that the attacks should continue. Part of the army had not yet been engaged and the Anglo-Spanish army was bound to collapse if more pressure was brought to bear. Marshal Jourdan did not see it that way. He felt the French army had already been badly mauled and should recuperate rather than attack. King Joseph agreed with Jourdan and flatly refused Victor's passionate appeals to attack again. Both King Joseph and Jourdan worried about an unfounded perception that the British might attempt a flank attack as well as reports from French cavalry scouts that there seemed to be increased activity from the Spanish troops. Evening was coming on and, in their view, the safest thing to do was to leave the field of Talavera and retreat to the east bank of the Albreche River. It was ordered accordingly. On receiving this order, Victor flew into a rage and fumed the whole evening; it was only at about 11 at night that he, his 1st Corps and the artillery left the Cerro de Cascajal. On the British side, every man was ready to 'drop down through fatigue and hunger', recalled Lt. Carrs of the 53rd adding that the soldiers 'had been under arms from 12 o'clock of the 27th ... without tasting anything stronger than water and that was very bad'. The battlefield was quiet again, except for the cries heard in the night of the desperately wounded men and the dying still strewn on the dark field.

LOSSES AT TALAVERA

The casualties at Talavera were amongst the highest recorded during the Peninsular War. Many senior officers were killed or wounded. Amongst the British, Maj. Gen. Sir Alexander Mackenzie, who had known Wellesley since boyhood as both had attended the Angers military school, and Brig. Gen. Langwerth had both perished. Major-General Hill and generals Henry Campbell and Alexander Campbell had been wounded. On the French side, Gen. Lapisse, one of the army's most experienced field officers, had been killed along with many other senior regimental officers.

The British army lost the following: killed, 34 officers and 643 NCOs and enlisted men; wounded, 196 officers and 3,719 NCOs and enlisted men; missing, 8 officers and 639 NCOs and enlisted men. Grand total: 5,363. The above figures are from Oman and Fortescue. In his 29 July dispatch, Wellesley mentioned 857 killed, 3,913 wounded and 653 missing for a grand total of 5,423.

For the Spanish army there are no detailed returns known. Gen. Cuesta stated that 1,201 men (including 51 officers, one of them Maj. Gen. Manglano wounded) were killed, wounded or missing, but without giving

Promoted on the morrow of Talavera. Watercolour by Lady Elizabeth Butler. (Anne S.K. Brown Military Collection, Brown University Library, Providence. Author's photo)

details. Considering that the Spanish army was not heavily engaged, the total of killed and wounded would have been at about 400 or 500 men at most by Sir Charles Oman's assessment, the balance being most likely the missing from the panic of Portago's division on 27 July. Thus, for the allies, the total casualties and missing came to about 6,600.

The French army lost 46 officers and 716 NCOs and enlisted men killed; 220 officers and 6,081 NCOs and enlisted men wounded; one officer and 205 NCOs and enlisted men missing for a grand total: 7,268.

According to Vérillon's *Les trophés de la France* (Paris, 1907), four 'English flags' were taken by the French at Talavera, including one by Maréchal-des-logis Legout-Duplessis of the 5th Dragoons who was said to have killed the ensign and put the colour guard to flight. There is, however, no British record of regimental colours being lost so these may have been plain flags or camp colours. Conversely, British memoirs by Leslie of the 29th Foot and Beamish of the King's German Legion mentioned that up to five colours or eagles were captured, but this was not certified by any actual trophy or official document, British or French, certifying these claims. The accounts mentioned that the poles had screw holes to fix eagles upon them; for the 29th, the two eagles would have been unscrewed and taken away while the three taken by the King's German Legion would have been presented to Wellesley. In the latter instance, it would have resulted in quite a fanfare in the press had such a thing occurred; the British forces had never yet captured any eagles from Napoleon's army. So, if they were not eagles, what were these poles and colours? Marshal Jourdan provided the answer when commenting upon the 'pretended flags or standards that Wellesley glories in having taken or destroyed. They are nothing more than small flags ('fanions') placed at the right and left of each battalion to keep the ranks aligned and that are thrown away by those who carry them when they have to use their weapons.' Thus, no eagles were lost at Talavera. The first eagle lost to British troops was at the battle of Barossa in March 1811.

AFTERMATH

FRENCH REINFORCEMENTS ON THE WAY

During the night of 28–29 July, King Joseph became increasingly worried about the safety of Madrid. Reports indicated that the corps led by Sir Robert Wilson was nearing Madrid from the west while a Spanish army had also appeared to the south-east, also seemingly heading for the Spanish capital. Indeed, while the battle of Talavera was being fought, Gen. Venegas had slowly moved up his army of La Mancha from the Guadiana River south-east of Toledo. This was done too late to prevent the gathering of Victor's, Sébastiani's and King Joseph's troops that faced the Anglo-Spanish army at Talavera, but Gen. Venegas caused much worry to the French all the same when he reached Aranjuez, north-east of Toledo, on 29 July. He was now some 40km from Madrid.

Thus, that night, once it had been determined that the badly mauled Anglo-Spanish army would not be making an attack the next day, King Joseph and Marshal Davout left Marshal Victor's 1st Corps of 18,000 men at the Albreche River to watch what the allies would do next while the rest of the French army hurried back to Toledo to protect it, as well as Madrid, from Gen. Vanegas and his Spanish troops.

Meanwhile, in the Anglo-Spanish camp, Brig. Gen. Robert Craufurd's Light Brigade had arrived at six on the morning of the 29th to reinforce Wellesley's army after a gruelling march, on which he and his men had travelled some 68km in 27 hours! Needless to add that all officers and men of the 40th, 52nd and 95th Regiments that made up the brigade were exhausted. But they were in excellent spirits and ready to fight.

The situation that Craufurd found at the HQ of the Anglo-Spanish army was anything but clear insofar as what the next step should be. General Cuesta wanted the combined forces to march on Madrid, which was the objective set by the Central Junta and Wellesley's original hope. It was also

Marshal Michel Ney, commander of 2nd French Army Corps. Temperamental in character, he could be an extraordinary tactician when calm, had a very quick mind in action and was a superb leader of men in battle. However, as Gen. Jomini observed, all these qualities diminished in proportion to commands that 'increased his responsibility' so Napoleon was careful to keep him as corps commander rather than make him an army commander. Portrait by F. Gérard painted in 1808. (Albany Institute of History and Art, Albany, NY. Author's photo)

Movements and engagements after the battle of Talavera

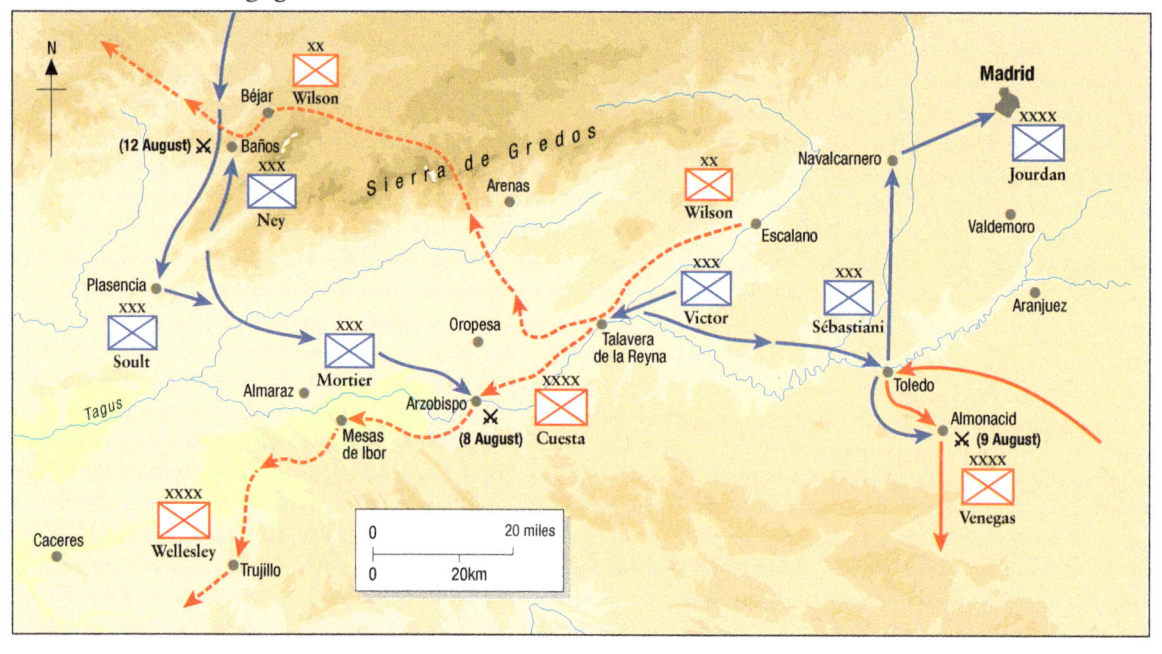

obvious that Gen. Cuesta also wanted to enter Madrid before his political rival, Gen. Venegas, could get there and thus reap the laurels of glory that would be showered on any Spanish army general that chased 'Pepe la Botella' out of the capital and sent him scurrying back to his imperial brother. It was a wonderful scenario, but the couriers arriving for Wellesley's attention were more sobering. Reports from scouts indicated increasing French troop movements in the area of Ciudad Rodrigo and these were confirmed on 30 July. It now became increasingly obvious that Gen. Soult's 2nd Corps of 18,000 men was moving south towards Baños through Leon and Estramadura, along with other bodies of French troops also coming through that area.

General Cuesta thus asked Wellesley to divert Sir Robert Wilson's force, which had been as far east as Escalona, west of Madrid, to race back to Baños to try to block or delay Marshal Soult's 2nd Corps while refusing to send a strong Spanish force as well. He wanted all his troops for the march on Madrid. After two days, he finally agreed to detach Gen. Bassecourt's division. By then, 2 August, it was learned that the French 2nd Corps had already passed Baños and marched into Plasencia, thus cutting the road west that had been used by the British army. Instead of marching on Madrid, Wellesley now wanted to march on Plasencia and deal with Soult's 2nd Corps that now appeared to the west. General Cuesta proposed to split the Anglo-Spanish army in two, one half at Talavera and the other moving on Plasencia. Early the next day, Wellesley learned that the French 2nd Corps was moving east and had reached Navalmoral.

Thus, for Wellesley, the situation was becoming clearer by the hour. Within a few days, a French corps would be able to cut off the route back to Portugal. Worse and then unknown in any detail by generals Wellesley and Cuesta, two more French corps, Marshal Ney's 2nd and Marshal Mortier's 5th, were also coming down to join Soult which meant that, within two weeks, up to 40,000 French troops might be blocking the road going west back to Portugal. And to the east, Marshal Victor's 1st Corps was within sight in a strong position on the far bank of the Albreche River. The short-term prospect was that Wellesley's army of about 18,000 able-bodied men thus risked being caught between Victor's 1st and Soult's 2nd Corps. That could, at worst, mean the destruction of the entire British army if it stayed at Talavera.

While the Spanish wished to liberate Madrid, the foremost objective of Wellesley's own political masters in London was to preserve the army he led. Should it be lost, the notion of keeping a field army in the Peninsula would possibly be rejected by the government and British public opinion. That would knock Portugal right out of the war as a viable military ally. The strategic options were thus very different for Wellesley than they were for his Spanish allies. If he could save his army, and that certainly was the wish of the British and Portuguese, the pressure would still be there for the French to contend with, and it could fight another day. The British army had to be saved.

On 3 August, captured French dispatches reached Talavera with the news that the 5th and 6th French corps were supporting Marshal Soult's 2nd Corps. This news changed the situation totally and Wellesley then made the decision to withdraw towards Portugal. On 4 August, generals Wellesley and Cuesta had a very tense meeting. As usual, Gen. O'Donoju translated Wellesley's decision. The starving British army was leaving Talavera. Some 2,500 British wounded had already been evacuated and some 500 eventually died on the way or were later captured by French patrols. Another 1,500 had to be left in Talavera to the mercy of fate. General Cuesta was of course extremely upset and felt betrayed at hearing that the British army was marching back to Portugal. He had envisaged attacking Soult's 2nd Corps by himself, but changed his mind and also left Talavera with his army heading west and crossed the Arzobispo bridge during the early hours on 6 August. There, he disposed his army to defend the bridge. Later that day, a new player came on the scene in the form of Marshal Mortier. His 5th Corps had reached the area and advanced towards the Arzobispo bridge, quickly scattering the rearguard of Gen. Cuesta's Spanish army. As soon as Marshal Mortier had appeared with his 17,000 men, Soult had tasked him with securing the Arzobispo bridge and Mortier, a no-nonsense efficient marshal, occupied the town of Arzobispo on 7 August and prepared his corps to attack the bridge.

On 8 August, Marshal Mortier ordered part of his force to ford the river, at a low level during the summer, at a crossing found further east and then waited until one in the afternoon when the Spanish, true to their habit, would take their daily siesta (or nap). Spanish sentries were awake and had earlier seen some French dragoons at the river watering their horses as they had done for the last few days. Suddenly everything changed: French cavalry and infantry attacked. The awakened and dazed Spanish soldiers formed squares

Marshal Mortier, commander of the 5th French Army Corps, c.1810. His troops crushed Gen. Cuesta's army on 8 August 1809 at Puente del Arzobispo. Scores of Spanish guns and colours were taken by the French. Contemporary print. (Anne S.K. Brown Military Collection, Brown University Library, Providence. Author's photo)

The Puente del Arzobispo, scene of Gen. Cuesta's defeat on 8 August 1809. This 'Archbishop's bridge' spans the Tagus River. Built in the 4th century, it still had its two distinctive and massive towers at the time of the Talavera campaign. The towers were later demolished. Contemporary print. (Private collection. Author's photo)

trying to resist while French artillery pounded the Spanish batteries. French dragoons cut many down until counter-attacked by the Duke of Albuquerque's cavalry, but the Spanish troopers had to retreat with Marshal Mortier's infantry coming into the battle. The Spanish field works were destroyed by French sappers and overwhelmed by infantrymen as was the bridge, in spite of gallant resistance by the Spanish infantrymen in its towers. The bridge taken, the French assaulted the Spanish batteries taking some 30 guns (including those taken by the El Rey Cavalry Regiment at Talavera). General Cuesta's army retreated south having lost some 800 men and another 600 having been taken prisoner by the French.

Marshal Victor's 1st Corps entered Talavera on 6 August and there found the 1,500 British wounded as well as many French wounded that had been rescued and cared for by the British medical personnel. Amongst these was Col. Meunier of the 9th Light Infantry, who recovered, and resumed his regimental command. Not only had the British medical personnel taken a very humane attitude towards the French wounded, they had also protected them as much as they could from Spanish soldiers and civilians who tried to rob and harm the helpless. The French were grateful and Marshal Victor made sure that both the French and British wounded would be cared for together and in the same way by his own medical staff. It was a remarkably humane event in a war that is remembered to this day for its atrocities.

Meanwhile, Gen. Venegas and his army of about 23,000 men with 40 guns were in the vicinity of Toledo. On 5 August, King Joseph and his troops with Gen. Sébastiani's 4th Corps reached Aranjuez and, three days later, entered Toledo, whose small Polish garrison in French service had been successful in courageously resisting the largely superior Spanish forces. The French now crossed the Tagus River and attacked Venegas at Almonacid. It was a Spanish disaster with the army of La Mancha almost destroyed, which gave the opportunity for King Joseph later to 'return triumphant to his capital' of Madrid commented Girod de l'Ain.

BAÑOS

Sir Robert Wilson and his Portuguese force had been detached from Plasencia on 11 July to provide cover to the north of Wellesley's and Cuesta's armies as they marched east towards Talavera de la Reyna. Wilson's detachment also went east but, by edging the northern bank of the Tiétar River until it came to the latitude of Talavera, turned south until it reached San Roman, about 15km north of Talavera, when it headed north-east edging the Albreche River heading towards Madrid. French scouts were trying to figure out where the fast-moving Wilson was and King Joseph was concerned about what might happen in Madrid if he ever reached it. The French knew that the Loyal Lusitanian Legion that he led had largely been responsible for the countless raids that had plagued them in Leon and Estramadura during the winter and spring as well as the remarkable defence of the Roman bridge at Alcantara against Marshal Victor (see *Oldest Allies: Alcantara 1809* in the Raid series). Now he and his redoubtable raiders were seemingly getting nearer to Madrid. This had been one of the factors convincing a worried King Joseph to march his guard back to his capital. Wilson had indeed reached Escalona, only about 60km from Madrid, when word came of developments elsewhere that dictated he should go back.

Wilson thus marched back in a westerly direction until he was in the Oropesa area, then turned north, crossed the Tiétar River and went into the mountains of the Sierra de Credos and turned west again heading for the pass at Baños. He loved to play 'cat-and-mouse' games with French formations that were much stronger than his forces, but, as he marched east, much of his luck was running out. He anticipated there would be a French force marching south through Estramadura that he could either try to block or delay at Baños, or even, follow its rear if it had passed already. The problem

The bridge at Puente del Arzobispo, early 21st century. The fine massive towers that were part of this structure at the time of the battle have regrettably disappeared. (Author's photo)

was that there now were three French corps in that area so the odds were heavily in favour of the French. By the time Sir Robert reached Baños on 11 August, both Marshal Soult's and Mortier's corps were further south. But Marshal Michel Ney's 6th Corps of some 15,000 with artillery was marching back towards the north and, on 12 August, it came into view of Baños and Sir Robert's force of about 3,000 Portuguese and Spanish troops.

They 'resisted the whole day, but had no guns, and were forced to retreat being surrounded' wrote William Warre, Portuguese Marshal Beresford's ADC, to his mother. This was the official version of the action. There were two reports of the affair, one false and public and the other accurate and secret. What really happened was later summarized by Wellesley to his brother William:

> The fact is that Sir Robert Wilson's action at Baños was nothing at all, excepting a dispersion, & a flight. He was marching through the pass with an intention of putting himself in communication with me again by Placentia. About 11 [in the morning] he saw a dust which he was informed was the enemy; & at about 5 [in the afternoon] he was attacked, & the Spanish troops instantly dispersed, (the Portuguese were not engaged) & he was himself pursued by the [French] cavalry for 8 miles, & escaped only by the swiftness of his horse. Colonel Grant the second in command was missing for 8 days; & a long time elapsed before the troops were again collected.

Marshal Ney's account confirms it. His troops quickly made contact with Sir Robert's force and the 'attack and success were equally rapid' largely thanks to an admirable charge by 3rd Hussars outside of Baños. Wilson disposed most of his troops on the heights at Baños, Ney brought up his artillery to pound the place followed by an assault by the 59th and 60th line infantry regiments that 'made themselves masters of the heights, which were obstinately defended'. Wilson rallied his men and counter-attacked but,

The battle at the Baños Pass in Estramadura, 12 August 1809. Marshal Ney's 6th Corps caught up with Wilson's much smaller Portuguese and Spanish force and scattered it. This print after S. Dascher in D. de Lonlay's *Notre Armée* (Paris, 1890) appears to be the only illustration of this last battle of the Talavera campaign. Unfortunately, it is highly inaccurate; British redcoats are shown (in the 1812–1815 uniform!), but none was present. Private Tartre of 59th French Line Infantry Regiment did indeed capture a colour. However, it was not British as shown, but Spanish. (Author's photo)

Ney reported, they were repulsed in a bayonet fight and scattered. Wilson reported losing about 400 men and Marshal Ney 190 French casualties. Back in England, Sir Robert claimed that his action at Baños was glorious, with his force delaying some 30,000 (!) French and saving many towns and British detachments as a result As time went on the story got better and there were hints that he had saved Wellesley from a surprise and eastern Portugal from invasion. Indeed, he sought the thanks of Parliament.

British field artillery train on the move, 1807. At Talavera, Wellesley's army was weakly provided with artillery. (Print after J. Atkinson Anne S.K. Brown Military Collection, Brown University Library, Providence. Author's photo)

NAPOLEON'S OPINION

Napoleon learned of the impending battle of Talavera when, on 7 August, a messenger arrived at the palace of Schönbrunn in Vienna bearing a letter from King Joseph dated 25 July in Madrid. It announced that Wellesley's and Cuestas' armies had made their junction. The Emperor immediately answered that he hoped King Joseph had taken proper measures to protect Madrid by forming an army of 55,000 men with 1st and 4th Corps and the Madrid garrison. This army, when joined to the 2nd, 5th and 6th Corps would then form a field force of about 100,000 men 'that would teach a lesson to the English and put an end to the war' in Spain. A few days later, he received a dispatch from King Joseph, written on 29 July, attesting that 'yesterday, the English army was forced [to evacuate] its positions. The battlefield upon which we are established is littered with their dead. I have one regret, sire, and that is not to have captured the whole English army.' Marshal Jourdan was equally optimistic and it sounded like a victory.

But Napoleon was not at all fooled by these first reports. More details of what had actually occurred at Talavera now arrived for his attention. These included the reports of the battle published in London newspapers. The British reports described a very different battle from the victorious affair related by Joseph and Jourdan. Napoleon flew into a rage!

On 18 August, in a letter to Minister of War Marshal Clarke, the Emperor's keen strategic eyes – he was one of the greatest strategists and tacticians of modern history – perceived 'what a fine opportunity we missed! 30,000 British [troops] some 150 leagues from the sea against 100,000 of the best troops in the world. My God! What is an army without a chief?' Three days later, he had more reports from the London newspapers and was now very angry. He advised Marshal Clarke to 'make it known to Marshal Jourdan my extreme displeasure regarding the inaccuracies and falsehoods that are in his reports; it is the first time the [French imperial] government is mocked in such a way ... my troops have been led to slaughter.' On 25 August, he complained further to Marshal Clarke that:

> The [battle's] account by the English general [mentions] that we lost 20 cannons and three colours. Testify to the king [Joseph] my astonishment, and my displeasure to Marshal Jourdan, in that I am sent folk tales ['carmagnoles'], and that, instead of informing me on the true situation, I am presented with boasts [worthy] of schoolchildren. I wish to know the truth. Who are the gunners that abandoned their pieces of artillery, [and] the infantry divisions that let them be captured? In your letter to the king, let him know that I was grieved to learn that he told the soldiers they are victorious; that [such statements will make us] lose [the trust of] the troops; that the fact is that I have lost the battle of Talavera; that I need to have reliable information, to know the number of killed, of wounded, of guns and colours lost.

Thus, as far away as Vienna, Napoleon had seen right through the smokescreen put up by King Joseph and Marshal Jourdan. His impeccable battlefield genius immediately came to the only possible conclusion: 'I have lost the battle of Talavera'.

That the Emperor was really very upset rather than having, as was sometimes his habit, a passing angry whim, is proved by what occurred during the next months. Marshal Jourdan was recalled and King Joseph stripped of any remaining real military powers. Seeing that the imperial mood was turning nasty, Marshal Victor weighed in. He already knew that King Joseph had asked Napoleon to recall both him and Marshal Ney. He made the point in that the French attacks on Talavera did not have the desired results because the reserve, mostly under the direct command of King Joseph, had not been committed. That was the sort of battle account that the Emperor wanted to see: no frills, just the facts as the local commander truly evaluated them. In any event, Napoleon was not really angry at marshals Victor, Soult, Mortier or Ney. Indeed, as late as 13 December 1809, Napoleon asked Marshal Mortier to write to Marshal Victor that he had 'no grudges against him for the affairs of Talavera'.

Marshal Jourdan became the prime French 'casualty' of Talavera. His sin was indeed considerable in that he had not accurately informed his commander-in-chief, who also happened to be his political master, about the true state of affairs. King Joseph had also been very optimistic, but Napoleon

The Iberian Peninsula, September 1809 to January 1810

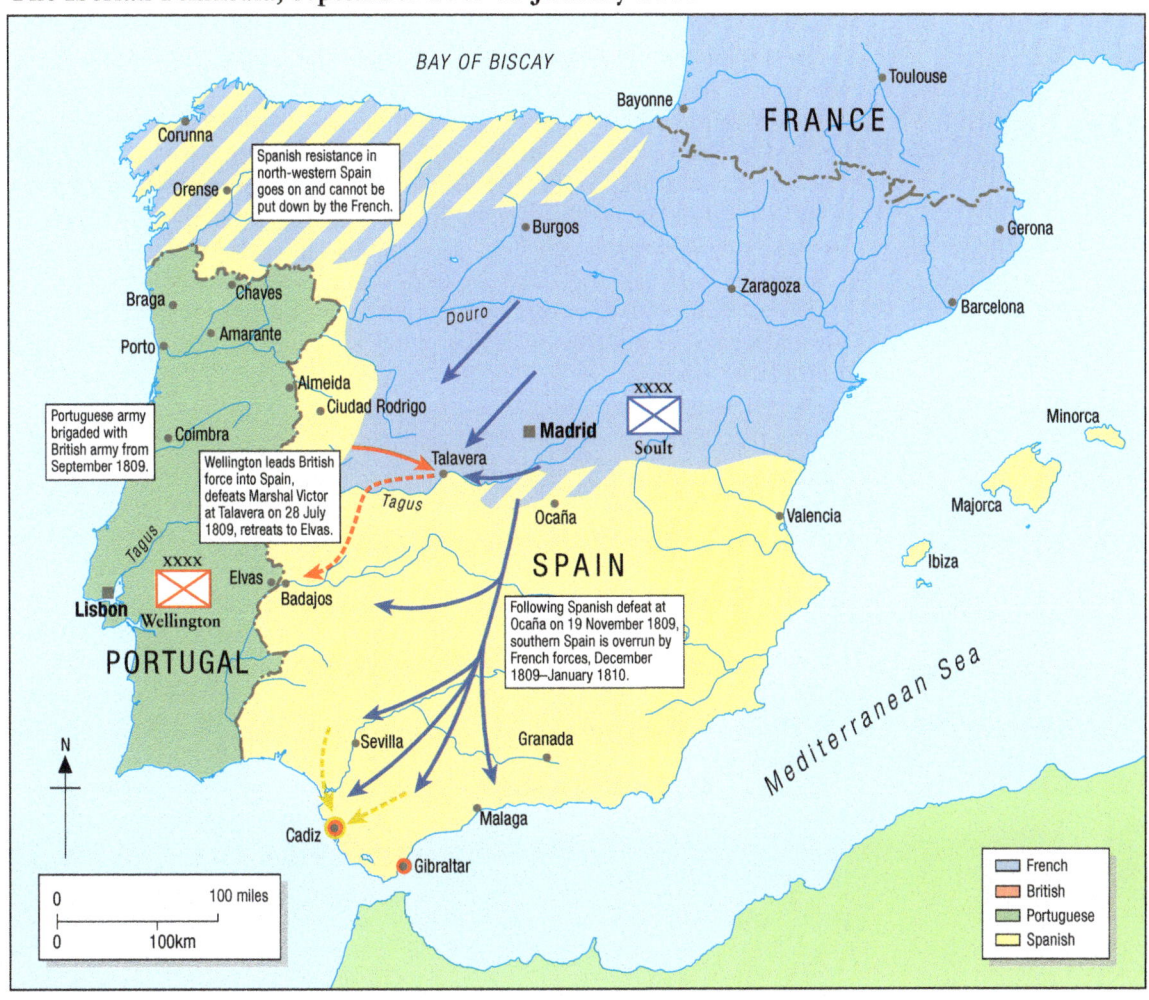

Map annotations:
- Spanish resistance in north-western Spain goes on and cannot be put down by the French.
- Portuguese army brigaded with British army from September 1809.
- Wellington leads British force into Spain, defeats Marshal Victor at Talavera on 28 July 1809, retreats to Elvas.
- Following Spanish defeat at Ocaña on 19 November 1809, southern Spain is overrun by French forces, December 1809–January 1810.

Legend: French, British, Portuguese, Spanish

---

knew that his brother was not a real soldier. Marshal Jourdan certainly was a military man and for him there could be no excuses. On 25 September 1809, the Emperor recalled him to France. Marshal Soult was appointed to replace him as the senior military officer in Spain. By this appointment, King Joseph was forced to step back into his place as the figurehead of the imperial regime in Spain; Soult and the other marshals actually ran the French forces and, henceforth, only they had Napoleon's trust.

Although he was assailed daily by a myriad of issues from all over Europe, Talavera was still on Napoleon's mind as late as 6 October 1809 when he wrote to Marshal Clarke about a report made to the Grand Duke of Baden's court in Karlsruhe by Gen. Sénarmont, the artillery commander at Talavera. General Sénarmont had, Napoleon wrote, 'reported on the bravery of the troops from Baden, etc. I find these reports extremely misplaced'. The Emperor had obviously not considered the foreign contingents nor the French artillery's performance at the battle to have been remarkable. Thus, three months after the event, Napoleon was still very upset about Talavera. So much so that, when the Grand Duke of Baden awarded Gen. Sénarmont the Great Cross of his order of merit, the Emperor forbade Sénarmont to wear it!

On 1 October 1809 the *Moniteur* pushed its propaganda message when, at the end of an article describing the monumental British fiasco at Walcheren, it made light of 'the great success' by Lord Wellesley, as proclaimed by British newspapers with regards to the battle of Talavera. The 'English people must have a great deal of recognition' because he managed

> To have part of his troops destroyed, to have compromised the glory of its arms, to have fled some 60 leagues, pursued with the sword to his back, and finally to have abandoned his [Spanish] allies. The king of England has rewarded these great services by granting [Wellesley] the title of Lord Wellington... Why was Lord Chatham [in command at Walcheren] not so honoured? Such a reward would be as well merited as the one awarded to Wellesley. We hope that the English general will be thrown into the Tagus River during the course of this winter and evacuate Portugal, [so that he will then] be granted the title of Duke of Lisbon.

Most of all, the Spanish people understood far better than most of their bickering leaders that if the British army in Portugal was destroyed, that would mean the end of their struggle to shake off the yoke of Napoleonic France and, in a sense, the end of the Iberia they knew and loved. Quite apart from all the arms and material help that Britain poured into the Peninsula, Wellesley's Talavera campaign had shown that the French occupation troops could never take things for granted with a British army in Portugal. One could hope of a future liberation. Thus, by Talavera, was hope maintained, kindled and expanded in the heart of Iberia's peoples.

THE BATTLEFIELD TODAY

The area of Talavera de la Reyna is easily accessible by car using the A5 motorway. Exit 118 to the city of Talavera de la Reyna has, on its north side, a large tripod memorial monument to the battle, erected once the motorway was built. Each span of the tripod commemorates one of the armies represented in the battle, the faces of each span being inscribed with the unit names of each army, British, Spanish and French, that fought there. A look at the ceramic tile map, which generally resembles that given in Fortescue's *History of the British Army*, reveals just how much the field of battle of 27 and 28 July 1809 has changed.

Most of the changes have occurred since 1945. That year, construction started to create a large irrigation reservoir by building a dam across the Portina River. During the battle, this river served as the 'frontier' between the opposing lines going from the town well into the hills. The Portina River has now all but disappeared while a large artificial lake has filled the

The centre of the battlefield of Talavera as seen from the south. On 28 July 1808, this general area was covered with British lines on the left (west) and French formation on the right (east) facing each other. Spanish troops were further south and further north. The grey cement fence of the motorway that now cuts across the field marks the beginning of the slopes leading to the hills seen in the background. The tripod memorial monument to the battle is at the centre. (Author's photo)

Monument to the battle of Talavera. The three elements of this large tripod memorial monument symbolize the armies of the three nations engaged in the battle. The names of the participating units are inscribed on each span. The monument was built in the late 1980s at the time of the construction of the Madrid–Sevilla motorway and is part of a driver's rest area at one of the Talavera exits. (Author's photo)

Northern Plain. Thus, much or all the positions held by Albuquerque's and Bassecourt's Spanish, Anson's and Stewart's British, and Ruffin's and Merle's French formations, as well as the area where the British cavalry charged, are now underwater.

When the author first visited the battlefield in the early 1980s, the dam was built and the Portina River's course had been changed, but the rest of the battlefield consisted mainly of agricultural fields. Following Spain's 1985 entry into the European Union, great infrastructure works started including the construction of the A5 motorway linking Madrid with Andalusia. In so doing, the motorway cut a wide swathe through the battlefield on the southern plain just below the Cerro de Medellin and Cerro de Cascajal. Furthermore, the city now enjoyed rapid urban expansion thanks to its improving economy that turned other parts of the southern plain into suburbs or industrial parks.

Still, the resolute traveller might want to wander into the back roads north of the motorway. One should have the latest detailed map giving local small roads and paths along with some patience and leisure time. Dead ends on dirt roads are frequent and there are no markers, except for the small stone memorial obelisk put up in 1909 on top of the Cerro de Medellin. The obelisk is now on private property and inaccessible, except by previous arrangement.

The town of Talavera de la Reyna is especially picturesque near the Tagus River and well worth a visit. There are some fine dining spots in that area. Going south-east on the A5 motorway, one is only about an hour away from Trujillo (the birthplace of Peru's conquistador, Pizzaro), the Medieval town centre of which has arguably one of the loveliest plazas in Spain. Again having drinks or a meal overlooking the plaza, just as many of the men that took part in the Talavera campaign did, is one of the pleasures of the latter-day dinner-table generals that we, who craft or read military books, all are.

Talavera de la Reyna, early 21st century. Urban development, warehouses and roads have, especially since the 1970s and 1980s, covered much of the battlefield right up to the hills of the Sierra de Segurilla to the north, from where this photo was taken. In the foreground, a road leading into the nearby Madrid–Sevilla motorway with power lines above, further away is suburban housing and the city's taller buildings that hide the Tagus River. Beyond are the hills that lead south into a mountainous region that was, at the time of the Peninsular War, a guerrilla's haven. (Author's photo)

FURTHER READING

The campaign of Talavera has been studied in much detail from the mostly British point of view in Sir Charles Oman's *History of the Peninsular War*, volume II of which, published in Oxford in 1903, was devoted to the events leading to this clash as well as to the battle itself and it remains an essential source. Much of this was reviewed in Sir John Fortescue's chapter on the battle in his *A History of the British Army* in its volume VII published in London in 1935 with good maps. Peter Edwards, *Talavera: Wellington's Early Peninsular Victories 1808–1809*, Crowood Press: Ramsbury (2005) is also highly recommended and brings in more aspects from British sources. Much of the primary source correspondence has been published in Lt. Col. Gurwood, ed., *The Dispatches of Field Marshal the Duke of Wellington*, London (1837), Vol. IV.

French studies on Talavera have been practically non-existent until the recent advent of historian Natalia Griffon de Pleineville whose *La bataille de Talavera, Espagne, 1809*, dossier Gloire & Empire No. 36, Coprur: Strasbourg (2011) not only reveals a mastery of the British sources, but further outlays a wealth of French correspondence (notably Marshal Victor's unpublished letters) and memoirs in their essential features as well as having a wealth of colour illustrations and maps. All this makes it an outstanding study, on par with Oman as a source.

Of the forces involved, the British army is well covered in Oman's *Wellington's Army*, London (1913) and in Philip J. Haythornthwaite's *The Armies of Wellington*, London (1994). Regimental histories of the various British regiments involved all cover their units' participation. Many works deal with Napoleon's troops but John Elting's *Swords Around a Throne*, New York (1988) is one of the best and most enjoyable to read. There are few works in English on the Spanish forces and we humbly list our own *Spanish Army of the Napoleonic Wars* (Osprey Men-at-Arms).

Spanish studies have, somewhat like the British, mentioned the battle in multi-volume works on the Peninsular War such as the late-19th-century *Guerra de la Independencia* by José Gomez de Arteche whose tome VI (Madrid, 1886) partly deals with the Talavera campaign. Juan José Sanudo Bayon's, 'La Batalla de Talavera 1809', *Researching & Dragons*, VII and VIII, Madrid (2002 and 2003) was also useful. These sources are in Spanish.

Other published works:
Correspondance de Napoléon 1er, Paris (1865), Vol. XIX
Díaz y Pérez, Nicolas, *Historia de Talavera la Real, villa de la provincia de Badajoz*, Madrid (1879)
Donkin, R. S., *United Services Journal*, July 1830
Hugo, A., *France Militaire*, Paris (1837), Vol. IV
Le Coustumier, Jacques, *Le Maréchal Victor*, Paris: Fondation Napoléon (c.2004)
Le Noble, Pierre, *Mémoires sur les opérations militaires des Français: en Galice, en Portugal, et dans la vallée du Tage, en 1809, sous le commandement du Maréchal Soult, Duc de Damatie*, Paris (1821)
Luz Soriano, Simao José da, *Historia da Guerra Civil*, Lisbon (1871), Segunda epocha, Tome II
Mayne, William and John Scott Lillie, *A Narrative of Campaigns of the Loyal Lusitanian Legion during the Years 1809, 1810 & 1811*, London (1812)
Mémoires du Maréchal Ney, duc d'Elchingen, prince de la Moskowa, Paris (1833)
Mémoires et correspondance politique et militaire du roi Joseph, A. Du Casse, ed., Paris (1857), Vol. VI
Mémoires militaries du maréchal Jourdan (guerre d'Espagne), écrits par lui-même, Paris (1899)
Napier, William P. F., *History of the War in the Peninsula and in the South of France*, London, (1832)
Life and correspondence of Field Marshal Sir John Burgoyne, Baronet, W. Wrottesley, ed., London (1873)
Smith, Digby, *Napoleonic Wars Data Book*, Greenhill: London (1998)
Stewart, Charles, Lord Londonderry, *Narrative of the Peninsular War from 1808 to 1813*, London (1829), Vol. 1
Weller, Jac, *Wellington in the Peninsula, 1808–1814*, London (1969)
Wellington, Arthur, Duke of, *Supplementary Despatches and Memoranda of Field Marshal Arthur, Duke of Wellington*, London (1871), Vol. 13.
Wellington, Arthur, Duke of, 'Some Letters of the Duke of Wellington to his brother William Wellesley-Pole', Charles Webster, ed., *Camden Miscellany*, Vol. XVIII, London (1948)

INDEX

References to illustrations are shown in **bold**.

Alberche River 41, 42, 43, 54, 59–60, 81, 83
Albuquerque, Duke of 36, 63, 74, 77; aide 77
Alcantara bridge 85
Almaraz bridge **34**, 36
Almonacid, battle of (1809) 14, 84
Alorna, Marquis de 5
Anglo-Spanish army 14, 38, 41; during battle 42, 53, 54, 63, 78; plans 27–28; *see also* British army; Spanish army
Aranjuez 81, 84
Arzobispo bridge 83–84, **84**, 85
Austria 10, 38; Austrians 27

Baden, Grand Duke of 89
Bailen, battle of (1808) **9**, 9, 13
Baños 82; action at (1809) 14, 85–87
Barossa, battle of (1811) 80
battlefield today **41**, **91**, 91–93, **93**; Cerra de Medellin **49**, 92; monument **91**, 91, **92**
Blake, Lt. Gen. Joaquim 16
Brazil 6, **7**, **8**, 8, 13
British army 19–21 *see also* Anglo-Spanish army
 artillery 54, 56, 58, 67, 73, 75, **87**
 after battle 82, 83
 at battle 54, 56–57, 78
 before battle 14, 42–43
 battalions of Detachments, 1st and 48th 48
 bayonet charges 58–59, 68–69
 brigades: 2nd 16; Cameron's 48; Campbell's 43; Donkin's 43, 44, 49, 53, 73; Stewart's 48, 53, 58, 74; Tilson's 53
 cavalry brigades: Anson's 42, 62, 74; Fane's 62, 74
 cavalry division 21
 commanders 15–16
 discipline 20
 divisions 20–21; Campbell's **55**, 66–67; cavalry 21; Mackenzie's 42, 43; Sherbrooke's 21, 42, 43;
 dragoons 20, **34**; Guards, 3rd **19**
 drill 20
 enters Spain 11, 14, 27
 evacuated at Corunna 11, 13, 55
 expeditionary force in Portugal 10, 11, 13
 Guards, 3rd Foot 66, 68–69, **77**
 Highlanders 48; 42nd, grenadiers **30**
 King's German Legion *see* German Legion, King's
 Light Brigade, Craufurd's 81
 Light Dragoons, 23rd 75, 76–77
 line infantry sergeant **19**
 losses at Talavera 78, 83
 Loyal Lusitanian Legion *see* Lusitanian Legion, Loyal
 march towards Talavera 40, 41, 42
 order of battle 24
 organization 19
 plans 27, 30–31, 35–38
 regiments 19
 Regiments of Foot: 7th 67; 24th, 2nd Bn 67, 69; 29th 48, 79–80; 31st, 1st Bn 69; 40th 67, 81; 45th, 2nd Bn 69; 48th **61**, **62**; 48th, 1st Bn 48, 69; 53rd 67, 78; 60th 19–20; 60th, 5th (Rifles) Bn **20**, 21, 57; 61st 68; 83rd 68; 87th and 88th 44–45; 95th 19–20, 81
 Royal Artillery officer **20**
 staff officers **34**
 wounded at Talavera 78, 83, 84
British shipyards 5

Cameron, Brig. Gen. 68
Campbell, Brig. Gen. Alexander 78
Campbell, Brig. Gen. Henry 67, 78
Canada 5
carabiniers 22–23, **42**
Carlos IV, King of Spain 7, 22
Carrs, Lt. 78
Casa de Miravete 14, 30–31
Casa de Salinas 42, 44–45, 53
Cataneo, Ensign Don Pablo **72**
Cerra de Cascajal 40, 43, 44, 54, 55, 56, 59, 66, 73, 77, 78
Cerra de Medellin 40, 42, 43, 44, 45, 48–49, **49**, **52**, 53, 55, 56, 57–59, 62, 63, 67, 69, 74, 75, 92
chasseurs 22–23, **42**
chronology 13–14
Cintra, convention of (1808) 10
Clarke, Marshal 88, 89
Close, Lt. 48
commanders, opposing 15–18; British 15–16; French 17–18; Spanish 16–17; *see also individual entries*
'Continental Blockade' 5
corporals **30**, **73**
Corunna 11; battle of (1809) 11, 13, 55
Cotton, Maj. Gen. Stapleton (later Lord Combermere) 57
Cradock, Maj. Gen. Sir John 11
Cuenca churches 8
Cuesta y Fernandez de Celis, Capt. Gen. Gregorio Garcia de La 14, **17**, 27, 41, 44, 77, 78–79, 81–82; at battle 56, 62–63, **72**, 81; distrust of British 35, 36; life and career 16–17; meetings with Wellesley 30–31, **34**, 35, 36, 83; plans 38

Dalrymple, Sir Hew 10, 15
Davout, Marshal 81
Dessolle, Gen. of Division Jean-Joseph **18**, 23, 59, 60
Donkin, Col. Rufane 77
Donnellan, Lt. Col. Charles **61**, **62**, 69
'Dos de Mayo' revolt (1808) 8, 13
dragoons, British **19**, **20**, **34**
Dundas, Sir David, drill instructions 20
Dupont, Gen. **9**, 9, 13

Eben, Baron 11
Elley, Lt. Col. 76, 77
Estramadura 14, 85

Fernando VII, King of Spain **7**, 7, 8, 13, 16, 36
forces, opposing 19–23; British 19–21; French 22–23; Spanish 21–22; *see also individual entries*
Fortescue, Sir John 78, 91
Franceschi, Gen. of Division **30**, **39**
French imperial army 22–23
 artillery 54, 56, 58, 66, 67, 73, 78; foot **23**, **29**
 Baden Regiment 67, **72**, **74**
 at battle 54, 56–57, 78
 before battle 42, 43, 44
 carabiniers 22–23, **42**
 cavalry, Merlin's 74
 chasseurs 22–23, **42**
 Chasseurs à cheval: 10th and 26th regiments 74–75, 76, 77; Imperial Guard **7**
 commanders 17–18
 contingents from allied states **23**, 23
 Corps, 1st (Victor's) 14, 29, 41, 42, 43, 74, 78, 81, 82–83, 84, 87; light artillery 44; attack 44–45, **46–47**, 48–49, 53; morning attack 56–59
 Corps, 2nd (Soult's) 11, 12, 14, 15, 29, 30, 37, 60, 61, 82
 Corps, 4th (Sébastiani's) 14, 23, 29, 38, 41, 44, 53, 55, 61, 63, 67, 84, 87

Corps, 5th (Mortier's) 14, 29, 37, 53, 60, 61, 82, 83–84
Corps, 6th (Ney's) 11, 14, 29, 37, 53, 60, 61, 82, 83, 86, 87
 defeats: at Bailen **9**, 9, 13; at Roliça 10, 13; at Vimiero 10, 13
 divisions: Dessolle's 23; Lapisse's 42, 56, 63, 67; Leval's **55**, 55, 63, 66, 67, 69, **72**, 73, 77; Ruffin's 43, 44, 45, 56, 59, 74–75; Valence's Polish (Madrid Garrison) 53, 60–61; Villatte's 56, 59, 73, 74–75
 Dragoon Division, 1st (Latour-Maubourg's) 56, 63, 69
 Dragoon Division, 2nd (Milhaud's) **22**, 55, 63
 dragoons 14, 43; elite company **22**
 drill 23
 Dutch regiments 23, 67; 2nd **68**
 Frankfurt Infantry Bn **23**, 67, 73
 grenadier **9**
 Hesse-Darmstadt battalion **23**, 67, 73
 Hessian Crown Prince Regiment **73**
 Hussars Regiment, 2nd **22**
 Imperial Guard 11; Chasseurs à cheval **7**
 infantry tactics 23
 light infantry regiments: 9th **42**, 45, 48–49, 56, 58, 63, 66, 74–75; 27th 74–75, 76
 line infantry regiments 22–23, **23**; 8th 68, 69; 24th 45, 56, 57–58, 74–75; 32nd 69; 54th 69; 59th and 60th 86; 63rd 74–75; 75th 69; 96th **43**, 45, 56, 58, 74–75
 losses at Talavera 78, 79
 march towards Talavera 40, 41, 42
 movements, July 1809 28
 Nassau Regiment 66–67
 order of battle 25–26
 organization 22–23
 plans 29, 55–56, 63
 Polish battalions 60–61
 Polish garrison at Toledo 84
 Polish Vistula Legion lancers 74–75, **75**, 76, 77
 Portuguese invasion 5–7, 10, 12, 13, 15
 regiments 22–23
 retreat from Portugal 8, **10**, 10, 13, 15
 in Spain 5, 7, 8–9, 10, 13, 40
 voltigeurs 21, 22, 23, 56, 73, 74, 75
 Westphalian Light Horse 74–75, 76, 77
 wounded at Talavera 79, 84
fusiliers **43**, **74**

German Legion, King's **19**, 21, 44, 49, 68–69, 79–80; artillery, Rettberg's battery 62, 63; battalion, 5th 45, 58; battalion, 7th 45; brigade, Langwerth's 43, 44, 45, 69; brigade, Löw's 43, 44, 45, 68; Hussars, 1st 75, 76; Light Dragoons, 1st **73**
Gordon, Lt. Col. 68
grenadiers **30**, **43**
guerrillas, Spanish **21**, 30
gunners, French foot artillery **29**

Heathfield, Lord 11
Hill, Maj. Gen. Rowland 45, 48, 49, 57, 78; life and career 16
Huguet-Châteaux, Col. 53

Iberian Peninsula: early to mid-1809 6; Sept. 1809 to Jan. 1810 89
infantrymen: British **55**; French **23**; Spanish **21**, **31**
Joao VI, Prince Regent of Portugal 6, **8**, 13
Joseph Bonaparte, King of Spain **5**; after battle 82, 84; at battle 53, 55, 56, 59, 60, 61, 78;

95

before battle 7, 8–9, 10, 13, 14, 18, 38, 41; dispatches to Napoleon 87, 88; life and career 18; reorganizes disposition of troops 29; and safety of Madrid 53, 56, 60, 81, 85; stripped of military powers 88–89; and Victor's attack 53
Jourdan, Marshal Jean-Baptiste 10, 14, **18**, 29, 41, 87, 88, 89; during battle 53, 55, 56, 59–60, 61, 78, 80; life and career 18
Junot, Gen. Andoche 5, 10, 13, 15, 55
Junta, Central 21, 27, 36, 81
'junta' governments 8, 21, 36

l'Ain, Girod de 48, 58, 63, 66, 84
Langwerth, Brig. Gen. 69, 78
Lapisse, Gen. 67, 69, 78
Lastres, Col. José de 69, **72**
Legout-Duplessis, Maréchal-des-logis 79
Leval, Gen. 66, 67, 69, 77
Lisbon 11, 13
Lusitanian Legion, Loyal (Wilson's force) 12, 14, 37, 81, 82, 85–87; Hussars, 3rd 86

Mackenzie, Maj. Gen. Sir Alexander 43, 49, 69, 78
Madrid 8, **9**, 9, 10, 13, 81–82, 84, 87; Garrison 14, 53, 60–61, 87; King Joseph's worries over safety 53, 56, 60, 81, 85; revolt, 'Dos de Mayo' 8, 13
Medellin, battle of (1809) 16
Medina del Rio Seco, battle of (1808) 16
Merlin, Gen. Antoine-François-Eugène **28**, 74
Meunier, Col. 49, 84
Middlemore, Maj. **61**, 69
Moniteur 90
Moore, Maj. Gen. Sir John 11, 13
Mortier, Marshal 83, 83, 88
Murat, Marshal 8
Myers, Lt. Col. 67

Napoleon I, Emperor of the French 5, 7, 8, 17, 18, 53; Austrian campaign 38; 'Continental Blockade' 5; and Iberian problem 10; opinion of Talavera 87–90; Portuguese invasion 5, 6–7; in Spain 10, 11, 13
Napier, William P. F. 48, 77
NCO, senior, King's German Legion 73
Ney, Marshal Michel 11, 14, **81**, 86–87
Northern Plain 40, 43, 62, 63, 74–78, 91–92; ravine 75–76

O'Donoju, Gen. Juan 31, **34**, 36, 83; life and career 17
officers: Dragoon Guards, 3rd **19**; French foot artillery **23**; Irlanda Regiment **21**; Polish Vistula Legion **75**; Royal Artillery **20**; *see also individual ranks*
Oman, Sir Charles 78, 79
orders of battle: British army **24**; French army **25–26**; Spanish Army **21–22**, **24–25**
Oropesa 14, 40

Pajar de Vergara 43, 63, 67, 69
plans, opposing 27–31, 35–38: British 27, 30–31, 35–38; French 29, 55–56, 63; Spanish 30–31, 35–38
Porbeck, Col. von 67
Portina River 40, 42–43, 54, 58, 63, 69, 91–92
Porto 5, 8, 12, 14, 15
Portugal 5, 12, 55, 83; British expeditionary force in 10, 11, 13; French invasion of 5–7, 10, 12, 13, 15; French retreat from 8, **10**, 10, 13, 15; revolt in 8, 13; royal family sails to Brazil 6–7, **8**, 8, 13
Portuguese army 5, 12 *see also* Lusitanian Legion, Loyal
Principe Real 6, **8**
privates: Foot, 60th **20**; fusilier, Baden Regiment **74**; grenadier, 92nd Highlanders **30**; Guards, 3rd Foot **77**; of *voltigeurs* **23**

Promoted on the morrow of Talavera 79
Puente del Arzobispo 83, **84**, 85; battle of (1809) 14, 83–84

Rio de Janeiro 6, 7, **8**
Roliça, battle of (1808) 10, 13
Ruffin, Gen. of Division François Amable 43, **48**, 77

Sébastiani, Gen. Horace **18**, 38, 55, 56, 59, 60, 67
Sénarmont, Gen. 89
sergeant, British **19**
Sherbrooke, Lt. Gen. Sir John Coape **16**, 43, 48, 58, 67; life and career 15
Sierra, Capt. Don Francisco de **72**
Sierra de Seguilla 40, 62–63, 74
Soult, Marshal Nicolas 11, 12, 14, 15, **27**, 30, 53, 55, 60, 61, 89
Spain: British troops enter 11, 14, 27; central, c.1810s–1820s **28**; French troops in 5, 7, 8–9, 10, 13, 40; Junta, Central/Supreme 21, 27, 36, 81; politics, state of 36; revolt in 8, 13; royal family 7
Spanish army of Estramadura 14, 16, 21–22, 56, 78; artillery 54, 75; at Arzobispo bridge 83–84; before battle 42–44; cavalry 14, 44, 69; Cavalry, Light **35**; cavalry division, Duke of Albuquerque's 63, 74, 84; commanders 16–17; courage and tenacity 73; defeated by French 14; Division, 3rd (Portago's) 79; dragoon regiments, Pavia and Villaviciosa **37**; efficiency 22, 31; El Rey Regiment 69, **72**, 73; English perception of 31, 35; gunners 54; indiscipline in 8, 44; Infante Cavalry Regiment **21**; Infantry Battalion, Canarias **21**; Infantry Regiment, Leales de Fernando VII **31**; infantrymen **9**, **21**; Irlanda Regiment **21**; losses at Talavera 78–79; Madrid Garrison 14, 87; march towards Talavera 40, 41, 42; order of battle 21–22, 24–25; organization 21; plans 30–31, 35–38; Portuguese invasion 5; reserve division, Bassecourt's 62–63, 74, 82; review by Wellesley 31, 35; revolt 8; staff officers 21, **34**; strength 21; *see also* Anglo-Spanish army; guerrillas, Spanish
Spanish army of La Mancha 27, 28, 38, 53, 56, 60–61, 81, 84
Spanish Imperial guard 23, 41, 44
Spanish patriots entering Madrid **9**
standard-bearer, Spanish **21**
Stewart, Brig. Gen. Charles 31, 41

Tagus River 40; Almaraz bridge **34**, 36; Arzobispo bridge 83–84, **84**, 85; upper 5, 39, 40
Talavera, battle of (1809) 11, 12, 42–45, 48–49, 53–63, **58**, **60**, **61**, **62**, **63**, 66–69, 73–78, 79–80
  battlefield today *see* battlefield today
  British secure the Cerro de Medellin 48, **52**
  Casa de Salinas building 42, 44–45, 53
  continuation, 28 July 54, 63, 66–69, 73–78; afternoon 55, **64–65**, 66–68; charge of Spanish cavalry Regiment El Rey 69, **72**, 73; French make yet another attempt 69, 73; meeting 59–61; northern sector 73–78, **76**; northern sector ravine 75–76; renewed attacks 62–63, 66–69; truce 59, 62
  evening of 27 July 44–45, **46–47**, 48–49, **52**, 53
  Foot Guards, 3rd, repulse French attack 66, 68
  losses 78–80, **79**; British 78, 83; French 79; regimental colours 79–80; Spanish 78–79
  sleepless night (27/28 July) 53–54
  Victor attacks 17, 44–45, **46–47**, 48–49, 53
Talavera campaign
  action at Baños 85–87; aftermath of battle 81–90; French reinforcements on way 81–84; movements and engagements **82**; Napoleon's opinion 87–90
  area of coming battle 39–41, **40**
Talavera de la Reyna 14, 39, 40, 84, 91, 92, **93**, 93; armies converge on **40**, 41; fields west of **41**; roads to 40–41
Toledo 41, 53, 60–61, 81, 84
troopers: French **22**; Polish **75**; Spanish **21**, 35, 37
Turner, Gen. **11**

Unett, Capt. George W. **20**
uniforms
  British army **20**; Dragoon Guards, 3rd **19**; Guards, 3rd Foot **77**; Highlanders, 42nd, grenadiers **30**; infantrymen **55**; line infantry sergeant **19**; King's German Legion **73**; Regiment of Foot, 60th **20**; Royal Artillery **20**
  French army **23**; Baden Regiment **74**; Dragoons, 2nd and elite company **22**; Dutch Regiment, 2nd **68**; Frankfurt Infantry Bn **23**; Hessian Crown Prince Regiment **73**; Hussars Regiment, 2nd **22**; Imperial Guard, Chasseurs à cheval **7**; Light Infantry Regiment, 9th **42**; Line Infantry **23**; Line Infantry Regiment, 96th **43**; Polish Vistula Legion **75**
  Spanish army **21–22**; dragoons, Pavia and Villaviciosa **37**; Infante Cavalry Regiment **21**; infantry **21**; Infantry Battalion, Canarias **21**; Infantry Regiment, Leales de Fernando VII **31**; Irlanda Regiment **21**; Light Cavalry **35**

Valence, Gen. 60–61
Venegas, Gen. 14, 27, 28, 36, 38, 56, 81, 82, 84
Victor, Marshal, Duke of Belluno (formerly Claude-Victor Perrin) 14, **17**, 29, 38, 41, 53, 84, 88
  at battle 17, 69, 74, 78; attack by 44–45, **46–47**, 48–49, 53; morning attack 56–59; on 28 July 55, 56, 59, 60, 61
  life and career 17
Vigo-Roussillon, Col. 68
Villatte, Gen. 77
Vimeiro, battle of (1808) 10, 13, 15
Vittoria 10; battle of (1813) 18
voltigeurs 21, 22, 23, 56, 73, 74, 75

Walcheren expedition (1809) 27, 90
Wales, Prince of (later Prince Regent; King George IV) 11
Warre, William 86
Waterloo, battle of (1815) 15, 16
weapons: artillery 23, 54, 56, 58, 66, 67, 73, 75, **87**; muskets **19**, 23; rifles, British **19–20**, **20**; sabres, French cavalry **23**; Spanish **22**; swords, British cavalry **20**
Wellesley, Lt. Gen. Sir Arthur (later Duke of Wellington): and action at Baños 86; after battle 82; at battle 55, 56, 58, 62, 67, 69, 74, 77, 78; before battle 43, 44; appointed viscount 14, 15, 90; at Casa de Salinas 42; decides to evacuate Talavera 14; establishes HQ at Badajos 14; life and career 15; and losses at Talavera 78; march towards Talavera 41; meetings with Cuesta 14, 30–31, **34**, 35, 36, 83; *Moniteur* report on 90; perception of Spanish army at review 31, 35; plans 27, 37, 38, 41; in Portugal 10, 13, 15; reorganizes forces 20, 21; in Spain 14, 15; and Victor's attack 48, 53
Wilson, Sir Robert 12, 14, 37, **38**, 81, 82, 85–86, 87

York, Duke of, mistress 27